EDWIN C. MORGENROTH
2721 Fifth Avenue
Corona del Mar, Calif. 92625

D0753483

FISHERMAN'S WHARF
MONTEREY, CALIFORNIA
373-3664
the 3 RINGS BOOK shop

THE WORLD IS NEW

JOEL S. GOLDSMITH

THE WORLD
IS NEW

London

GEORGE ALLEN & UNWIN LTD

RUSKIN HOUSE   MUSEUM STREET

FIRST PUBLISHED IN 1962

SECOND IMPRESSION 1970

This book is copyright under the Berne Convention. All rights are reserved. Apart from any fair dealing for the purpose of private study, research, criticism or review, as permitted under the Copyright Act, 1956, no part of this publication may be reproduced, stored in a retrieval system, or transmitted, in any form or by any means, electronic, electrical, chemical, mechanical, optical, photocopying, recording or otherwise, without the prior permission of the copyright owner. Enquiries should be addressed to the publishers.

PRINTED IN GREAT BRITAIN
BY COMPTON PRINTING LTD.
LONDON & AYLESBURY

> Except the Lord build the house, they
> labour in vain that build it.
>
> Psalm 127

Illumination dissolves all material ties and binds men together with the golden chains of spiritual understanding; it acknowledges only the leadership of the Christ; it has no ritual or rule but the divine, impersonal, universal Love, no other worship than the inner Flame that is ever lit at the Shrine of Spirit. The union is the free state of spiritual brotherhood. The only restraint is the discipline of Soul; therefore, we know liberty without licence; we are a united universe without physical limits, a divine service to God without ceremony or creed. The illuminated walk without fear—by Grace.

THE INFINITE WAY

CONTENTS

CHAPTER I

CREATIVE MEDITATION

WE are all unfolding states of consciousness, and our outer experience will never be any greater than our inner unfoldment. Therefore, the only hope we have for better health, increased success, and more harmonious human relationships lies in the development of our consciousness. So unless by a week from now we have grown spiritually to a point beyond where we are today and our consciousness has been enriched, changed, or has reached a higher level, our demonstration of life and its harmonies will not be any more satisfying or better than it is now. Today then should be the beginning of a period of spiritual unfoldment which will be evidenced to the world by the fruitage in our lives.

Only one thing can bring this spiritual consciousness to us, and that is the realization of the presence of God in us. Before that presence of God can be realized, however, and our real consciousness come through, we must learn to still the human mind and the activity of the human senses to a degree which will permit us to become *consciously* aware of the presence of God, *consciously* aware of the divine Activity in, through, and as us—*as our consciousness*. God, the divine Being individualized as the Christ, becomes our individual consciousness, and that consciousness is the saviour of our world. That consciousness will lift our world up from the material sense of existence into spiritual reality.

This process of stilling the activity of the human mind and senses is known as meditation, and although meditation of itself is but a means to an end, the end is to achieve the spiritual life. As human beings, we have become separated from our Source. That is what makes us *appear* as human beings. We have turned a divine and spiritual experience into

a material one and have *finitized* that which is really the life
of God made *manifest as you and as me.* But when consciousness has been opened and the Christ has entered, we
can say with Jesus, and really mean it, 'I can of mine own
self do nothing[1] . . . the Father that dwelleth in me, he doeth
the works'.[2] The purpose of meditation, therefore, is to open
consciousness to the inflow of the Christ so that it becomes
spiritualized, the very Christ Itself in individual expression.

In creative meditation, the seed is planted so that the
creative Principle can act upon it and produce fruit after Its[3]
own kind. Instead of being cluttered up with the idea of
demonstrating something in the realm of effect—some expected form of material good—consciousness must be receptive and responsive to Truth, open to God and to the unfolding of the divine Consciousness. Therefore, let us above all
things be expectant of a greater degree of spiritual understanding, and for that very reason expectant of more harmony
in what we call our human experience which in reality is not
a human but a divine and spiritual one.

Stilling the human senses or the human mind, however,
does not for a moment mean trying to stop our thinking pro-
cesses because no one has ever succeeded in doing that. But to
those who practise meditation there does come a time when
the human mind of itself stops and extraneous thoughts no
longer intrude during meditation. This cannot be brought
about, however, through trying to stop thinking because all
we can do is to dam it up for a little while, and then it breaks
out stronger than ever. What we can do during meditation is
to learn to pay no attention to the thoughts that are passing
through our mind because these human thoughts will neither
harm nor help us. As a matter of fact, we learn in this work
that no amount of human good thinking will help and no
amount of human evil thinking will hurt.

[1] John 5: 30.   [2] John 14: 10.

[3] In the spiritual literature of the world, the varying concepts of
God are indicated by the use of such words as 'Father', 'Mother',
'Soul', 'Spirit', 'Principle', 'Love', 'Life'. Therefore, in this book the
author has used the pronouns 'He' and 'It', or 'Himself' and 'Itself',
interchangeably in referring to God.

Parenthetically, I must add at this point that there are some metaphysical teachings that emphasize the importance of 'right thinking', 'good human thinking', or 'learning to hold the right thought', and when I tell you that no amount of human good thinking will help and no amount of human evil thinking will hurt, I want to make clear that it is in no sense a criticism, judgment, or condemnation of any other approach to the spiritual life. Most of the paths that people take in their search for a better way of life lead them forward, on, and up to the final goal which is God. Therefore, I am not speaking in criticism of any other approach, but merely presenting what has been my individual unfoldment, which is that the human mind is not a power. The human mind cannot create good and it cannot create evil. True, it appears to do so, but that is only the *appearance* of good or of evil, and in some way, that appearance must be corrected.

Two times two is four, and no amount of human thinking will ever change that. Love is love, and nothing will change that. It is not the intention or object of this work to use the mind as a power to make something happen, but to attain a state of receptivity so that the Christ may flow in. That is why we meditate. That is what we hope to attain—the ability to achieve a conscious realization of the presence of God.

When the Christ becomes the reality of our being, we are then no longer in the human sense of existence, but in the spiritual. The first step on this path is to take our thought off person, place, and thing, off body, health, money or employment, off every human situation right now, this minute, and send it up to God—right now centre our thought on God.

And what is God? If anyone could define God, it would not be God, and therefore, we are not going to attempt to do that. Instead, we are going to centre our attention on the word God and remove thought from person, place, and thing:

God, the divine Consciousness of my being! God, the Soul of my being! God, the Law of my being! God, the Substance of my being—the Substance of all form! God, the creative Principle of the universe, the Law unto my being! God, the Substance,

*the Law of all form, of all formation! God, the Substance, the
Law, the Cause, and even the Form of all effect! God, the Substance, the Law, and the eternal Life of all form. God, Life,
cannot be separated from Its form, which I am.*

*God is the Spirit and Soul of my form. God, appearing in-
dividually as me, constitutes all there is of me. God is the life
of me, and that is why I am immortal—and immortal now.
Because God is the substance of my body, even my body is
immortal and spiritual. My body is not flesh and blood as it
appears to be. My body is as spiritual and immortal as my life
which is God.*[4]

In this meditation, we are not thinking of form, figure, outline,
colour, grace, or thinking anything else about the body. We
are thinking of God as the Substance of all form, colour, grace,
and outline—as the Substance of the body.

There is no reason for the body to ache, change, decay, or
die. We permit this to happen because of our acceptance of the
belief of a selfhood apart from God. We permit it because,
while we believe that God is the form and substance of *spiritual*
creation, we do not accept God as the form and substance of
all creation. But nevertheless God is the form, the substance,
and the law of all creation, including our body. Our body is
not material, nor is the food we eat material. It is spiritual. It
is only our concept of creation that is material. Creation itself
is God—God in the sense that God is its essence, substance, and
form. God is the substance of our being.

God is the substance of all being; God is the substance even
of a stone. God is the substance of the stars and the planets,
and the law unto them. The stars and the planets move according to an unchanging law, but they are not a law unto themselves. God is the law unto them, just as God, the divine Con-

---

[4] The italicized portions of this book are spontaneous meditations
which have come to the author during periods of uplifted consciousness and are not in any sense intended to be used as affirmations,
denials, or formulas. They have been inserted in this book from time
to time to serve as examples of the free flowing of the Spirit. As the
reader practises the Presence, he too, in his exalted moments, will
receive ever new and fresh inspiration as the outpouring of the Spirit.

sciousness of our being is the law unto us; but because we are infinite consciousness, the sun, moon, stars, and planets are embodied in us, and that same consciousness which we are is the law unto them.

My divine consciousness, imbued with the Christ, is the law unto all creation. Nothing in this world acts upon me. I am the law unto all that appears in my universe. The activity of God, the universal I, the one Ego, individualized as me, is the law unto all creation.

In creative meditation, our entire consciousness is filled with God—God as the Law, God as the Substance, God as the creative Principle, and God appearing as effect, as form, God appearing as sun, moon, and stars, God appearing as food, as pets, and as all relationships on earth. While our consciousness and thought are centred on God, such human thoughts as may come and go are of no importance, and therefore we do not try to stop them or to get rid of them. We let them come and go, and eventually they will fade away. This, however, is a matter of practice.

Let us recognize then that our reason for being on the spiritual path is so that we may become consciously aware of the presence of the Christ and become that I AM THAT I AM —the light of the world. Let us dedicate ourselves to that now. To attain that state of consciousness, I, myself, went through three months of inner initiation which took place every morning from five to seven. This was a magnificent experience and one that can never be shared wholly with anybody. In that period, it was shown to me that the only purpose of our existence on earth is to be the light of the world, to be a way to show others who are seekers, how to rise above the human sense of existence.

Everyone in the human world is faced with the belief of a physical body as well as with the belief of the need for material supply, and right now we are all being faced with the fear of atomic bombs and rumours of war. In the human picture, there is no way to avoid these experiences or to rise above them.

There is only one way to find safety and security, and that is the spiritual way, the way whereby the Christ becomes the reality of our being.

When we begin to look out from the standpoint of God, then we are living the Christ-way and fulfilling the greatest law ever revealed by Christ Jesus, the law of forgiveness, which is possible only as we live in obedience to the two great Commandments: 'Thou shalt love the Lord thy God with all thy heart, and with all thy soul, and with all thy mind . . . And . . . thou shalt love thy neighbour as thyself.'[5] That neighbour is every human being on earth, every animal, and every plant, but there is no way in which we can love them while holding them in condemnation.

We must see and understand that God is the life, Soul and mind, not only of our friends but of our so-called enemies. In that way, we eliminate all enemies. The answer to enemies or enmity of every form, whether appearing as man, sin, disease, or lack, is found in Jesus' reply to Pilate: 'Thou couldest have no power at all against me, except it were given thee from above.'[6]

The law of forgiveness, that is, the ability to see God as the mind, the life, and Soul of enemies as well as of friends, is the real law of demonstration. Not only in the Old Testament, but throughout the teachings of Jesus, the first Commandment is recognized as the secret of life—only one God, only one life, the life of every one of us, enemy or friend. God is the only mind, and therefore God must be the mind even of those we call enemies—only one God, only one creation, and all spiritual.

As long as our consciousness is filled with this oneness—one God, one creation, all one—our consciousness is open to the inflow of the Christ. There is no other way. Love is the way, and love is truth, and truth is the ability to become aware of God as the form and formation, the cause and effect of all that appears as our world. Thus our objective is embodied in these statements: 'The world is new to every soul when Christ has

<hr>

[5] Matthew 22: 37, 39.   [6] John 19:11.

entered into it.'[7] 'I can of mine own self do nothing[8] . . . the Father that dwelleth in me, he doeth the works[9] . . . I live, yet not I, but Christ liveth in me.'[10]

Sit in the silence, paying no attention to your thoughts, and take into your consciousness any or all of these ideas as your central theme. When you have finished, you will feel that you have become one with the divine Source of your being.

Those of you who have read The Infinite Way are familiar with the illustration found there on the subject of supply, in which it is pointed out that the oranges growing on the orange tree are not supply, they are not even the supply of oranges! They are the effect—the result or the fruitage of supply. Supply is the law that operates in and as the tree. Even if all the present crop of oranges were taken away, as long as that law is in operation, there will be oranges. For us to think of the oranges as supply and try to hold on to them or to give them away and think we are thereby giving away our supply is foolish because in due time there will be another crop of oranges.

With that illustration in mind, we can remember that everything we see is the result of the law of God. Behind the visible, is the law of God producing and reproducing. That which is visible to us, whether money or anything else, is but the effect of supply. It is not supply. It is only an *effect* of supply. Supply is the consciousness of good within, and as long as we have that we have the necessary dollars.

In exactly the same way, we look at people, but we do not think of them as good or bad, sick or well. We look *through* the person and see that every individual is the vehicle through which, or as which, God is appearing, and even while being grateful for the good that appears to come *through* him, we look behind the good to see the actual Source from which it comes.

No one is good of himself. Every bit of good we have ever done has not been as a result of our own nature at all. It has

[7] From an inscription in the chapel at Stanford University, Palo Alto, California. Source unknown.
[8] John 5:30.   [9] John 14:10.   [10] Galatians 2.20.

B

been God shining through. Of ourselves, we have never been charitable or kind. Charitableness and kindness are qualities of God. Similarly, evil is not a quality in and of itself either. It is our *misinterpretation* of reality that causes any person or thing to appear to us as evil. There cannot be the First Commandment, 'Thou shalt have no other gods before me'[11]—and evil. There cannot be infinite good *and* evil. So the evil we behold is only a negative appearance, concept, or false idea of that which is real, that which is God, Good.

And so, as we look at a person, let us look through him and see that only God is appearing through him, or as him; and the same with oranges, dollars, or with anything else. Let us not look upon them as supply, but as the effect of the law of God, which we are, and of God as the only power to any and every effect.

[11] Exodus 20:3.

CHAPTER II

UNFOLDING THE HEALING
CONSCIOUSNESS

WHEN John was in prison, he sent word to Jesus, 'Art thou he that should come, or do we look for another?'[1] In other words, he was asking, 'Is this the promised Messiah?' Jesus did not answer him by saying that he had been authorized or ordained or that he had received a licence to be a rabbi. He said, 'Go and shew John again those things which ye do hear and see: The blind receive their sight, and the lame walk, the lepers are cleansed, and the deaf hear, the dead are raised up, and the poor have the gospel preached to them.'[2]

The work of healing through the Spirit, however, is never the healing of a body or of any physical condition, even though it appears as the healing of the problems of human existence. That is the result, but it is not the work. The real work is the spiritualizing of consciousness and of thought, and the opening of consciousness to the receptivity of God.

The Infinite Way does not teach that there are no human problems: It teaches that *in the presence of God* there are no problems, and so when we stand in the conscious awareness of the presence of God, there is no poverty, sin, disease, or death to overcome. One of the greatest of all Jesus' statements is, 'Seek ye first the kingdom of God, and his righteousness; and all these things shall be added unto you.'[3] The kingdom of God —the realm of God—is consciousness. The spiritual atmosphere of God is the Kingdom, and when we are in the spiritual atmosphere of God, all the harmonies of heaven and of earth are added unto us.

There are many approaches to the subject and practice of

[1] Matthew 11:3.   [2] Matthew 11:4, 5.
[3] Matthew 5:33.

healing work, but I can speak only of that which has revealed itself to me, which is that *healing is accomplished entirely through silence*. Treatments, oral explanations, and the written word are merely little ladders which we use to climb up to the point of silence. Sometimes they are necessary, more often they are not.

After one has been in this work for a while, it is almost entirely unnecessary to use the mental argument in healing. It is possible just to close the eyes and quickly get into an atmosphere of silence and watch the healing take place. With practice, that silence becomes such a continuous experience that later on it is maintained consciously even while doing the every-day things of life—driving a car, writing, reading, housekeeping, or gardening. It is possible to maintain that spiritual atmosphere regardless of what is apparently being done by our body or mind.

Healing takes place whether or not we are actually engaged in the work of bringing it about, if our consciousness is anchored in God. Such was the atmosphere of Jesus' consciousness when the woman pushed through the throng. He did not know she was there seeking a healing, but she was healed simply by coming into the atmosphere of that consciousness, and doing so in faith.

In my writings, I have made it very clear that ninety-nine per cent of the responsibility for the healing work rests with the practitioner of spiritual healing, because healing is accomplished through a spiritual state of consciousness. Let me repeat that: *Healing is accomplished through a spiritual state of consciousness*. The practitioner, therefore, who lives, works, and has his being in that spiritual atmosphere will do beautiful healing work, and he will do it in proportion to the degree in which he dwells in this atmosphere. Although it is possible to bring forth healing even while being part of the human sense of life, to do the really great works, it becomes necessary to come out and be separate, to come out and live on a higher plane.

This does not mean that one cannot enjoy a movie, good music, family life, and a home, but it does mean that in a truly spiritual life the things of the human realm have little or no place even though the wonderfully sweet things in human life can be enjoyed without coming down to the level of much of this world's pleasures and pains. And so from the practitioner who lives in the highest degree of spiritual consciousness will emanate the highest kind of spiritual atmosphere, and he will do the best healing work.

This atmosphere has no relationship at all to sanctimoniousness. As a matter of fact, there may be some question as to how much spirituality the sanctimonious person has because true spirituality is always humble. Whether of the Master of two thousand years ago, or a minister, rabbi, or priest of today, one mark of true spirituality is the recognition that we are all one under the skin. Moreover, spirituality has nothing whatsoever to do with the amount of religious learning anyone has or professes to have. True spirituality has to do primarily with the degree in which one has realized the nothingness of evil and the presence of the Christ.

True spirituality begins with the realization of an inner Presence, an inner Power, and when that comes, it brings with it the other end of the same stick—the realization that what appears as sin or disease is not power: It is the universal belief of a selfhood apart from God; it is the accumulated human beliefs of the world.

All these banded together form a mental influence so strong as to become almost mesmeric, and when we see tracks coming together, the sky touching the mountain, or a snake where a rope really is, it is not surprising that we wonder what kind of miracle-performing treatment will change these appearances into their reality; but none of our prayers or treatments will ever change the streetcar tracks, the sky sitting on the mountain, or the rope that looks like a snake. Our treatment is the realization that the tracks are already normal and straight, that the sky has never sat on the mountain, that the rope has never been other than a rope: That realization of the nothingness of error is the second part of the revelation that comprises spiritual consciousness.

When we no longer hate or fear error in any form, when

we no longer love it, then we shall find that we have attained at least a great enough measure of spiritual consciousness to begin doing healing work.

And what is the patient's part in all this work? First of all, the patient makes it very difficult for himself and for the practitioner when he persists in maintaining the same attitude when going to a practitioner as he would when going to a doctor, when he acknowledges a physical disease to be his problem and then expects something to cure or remove it. In approaching a practitioner for healing, the attitude that is most helpful is: 'Show me how to find the Christ. I know that whatever of sin, discord, or disease may be present in my thought, or in or on my body, represents only that degree of the absence of the conscious awareness of God. Open this truth to me. Show me the presence of God. Reveal the omnipresent Christ that already is my own consciousness but of which I am not yet aware.' And so the attitude of the patient should be not to describe all the symptoms but rather to open consciousness to a receptivity to truth, to the presence of God.

That is the kind of co-operation which should first of all come from the patient who approaches a practitioner for healing, accompanied of course by a willingness to try insofar as possible to keep thought away from the problem and on the spiritual things of life. 'Thou wilt keep him in perfect peace, whose mind is stayed on thee'[4]—and that is not merely a biblical quotation. That is the actual truth. God does keep us in physical, mental, moral, and financial peace in the degree that our thought is turned away from the problems of life and centred on the spiritual realities.

And how can we do that? That comes about through contact with a teacher or practitioner with some measure of spiritual consciousness to whom one can turn to be lifted up. 'And I, if I be lifted up from the earth, will draw all men unto me.'[5] It is the practitioner's responsibility to stay on that high level day and night so that everyone who turns to him may be lifted up immediately into that consciousness wherein he is

[4] Isaiah 26:3.
[5] John 12:32.

able to discern spiritual perfection manifested as health, harmony, and supply.

It is also important in the development of spiritual awareness to read and study spiritually inspired literature. There now is a sufficient amount of such writing to appeal to every taste and on the level of every state of consciousness, and therefore everyone can find that which satisfies his own state of thought. There are those who respond only to the highest spiritual type of literature, only to that which keeps their consciousness high in God. There are others who are just as earnest seekers and just as desirous of finding God, but they cannot as easily accept that type of literature and therefore, they turn to writings of the more mental type which require a greater use of the thinking and reasoning process. There are also those who prefer that which will centre their thought on prayer and devotion. It does not necessarily follow that what has been recommended to a person by someone else will meet his need. Each person should find the literature that meets his particular need and is most suitable for him.

So it is important for the one who is seeking truth and healing to keep his thought on a high plane of consciousness and as much as possible away from the average radio and television programme, the grosser type of reading, and the typical moving pictures, and to lift himself up to the spiritual and mental plane which will help keep his consciousness open and receptive to the inflow of God.

There is a third point, too, which is important in the unfoldment of consciousness, and that is for those who are seeking truth to associate as much as possible with others on the same path. Few things are more helpful to progress on the spiritual path than meeting together. 'Where two or three are gathered together in my name, there am I in the midst of them.' When people come together seeking nothing from one another, with no thought in their minds but receptivity to the Christ, in that attitude and atmosphere, the Christ is in their midst to fill their need.

Those who attend such meetings do not do so for the purpose

6 Matthew 18:20.

of getting something, because they know that there is nothing of a material nature to be gained. There is only an atmosphere of the Christ for all to share. When there is a meeting together in that attitude of expectancy, that attitude of a consciousness open to God, what can result but good? And so every meeting we can have together on this level of spiritual thinking is helping to advance our progress.

Healing has nothing to do with any kind of process: Healing work has to do with the degree of silence attained. Sin, disease, and lack are unrealities; they have not, and never have had, a causative principle any more than the mirage on the desert has ever been found to be real water or a real city.

God, Soul, is the only creative principle; therefore, all that can ever have real being is the effect of God. All that exists in the realm of sin or disease must necessarily exist as an illusion or false sense which we are accepting. Knowing this, we understand that when we turn to the Christ for healing we are not really going to God for anything of a physical nature, we are not praying that God take away this disease or sin. We are going to God, the eternal Spirit, in order that Its divine, omnipresent wisdom may dissolve the illusion of sense for us, the illusory picture which at the moment is appearing as sin or as disease.

The things of God are foolishness with men just as 'the wisdom of this world is foolishness with God.'[7] We do not go to God to tell Him what disease is to be removed, what sin, or what lack or limitation, nor do we go to God to explain our need for money or for employment. We go to God for but one purpose—to hear the still small voice—and if we have any other purpose, let us drop it right here and now. If we have a sin or a disease that God could remove. He should have removed it long before we ever prayed for help, and if He has not done so without our asking Him, then God would not be God but a brute. The fact, then, that we still have a problem is proof that we do not have a problem that God could have done something about or can do something about.

The point—and this is very important—is that what we are entertaining is a false sense of God and God's creation. There

[7] I Corinthians 3 : 19.

is only one place we can go to have that corrected and that is to God, but we do not go to God for the purpose of telling Him that our need is physical, mental, moral, or financial. It is not necessary in any way to try to enlighten God as to the nature of our problem, nor to explain it even to the practitioner. In this approach to spiritual healing, diagnosis plays no part. It is never necessary to tell a practitioner where the pain is, what organ is affected, or even the name of the person requiring help. We must remember that the practitioner, too, can of his own self do nothing.

Now let us ask ourselves: If we of our own selves had the power to heal anyone, would we not be doing it this very minute instead of spending time talking about it? There is nothing that we can do of our own selves, and certainly we are in the same position in which Jesus was when he said that he could do nothing of himself. But the Father within, this spiritual Consciousness, this divine Spirit, can and does dissolve every appearance of error. Every form and every phase of discord are overcome, destroyed, and eliminated by the conscious realization of the presence of God. And so let it be remembered by both practitioner and patient that the healing work is done through the silence, but not necessarily through sitting with eyes closed and waiting for God to do something because that is not always silence, although sometimes it may be a good preparation for it.

Silence is a state of receptivity, a conscious awareness of our own being, whether with eyes closed or open—even when washing dishes, pounding a typewriter, or managing an office. Silence is a state of being when consciousness is alert and the ears are open and receptive for that still small voice. We prepare for that state of receptivity, for that state of conscious awareness, by going into meditation or into the silence when we awaken in the morning, turning within before we are out of bed, remembering, 'I live; yet not I, but Christ liveth in me.'[8] Thus we open the way right then and there for the Christ to be the guiding point of consciousness, the healing Influence throughout the day. To make room for this healing Influence

[8] Galatians 2:20.

upon awakening in the morning, the first thought should be to open consciousness to the inflow of the Christ, to the Father within.

When we begin our meditation with a statement or quotation, we should give the words we use a specific meaning of our own. There is nothing more harmful than the use of quotations repeated over and over again because they can become hypnotic in their effect and will result in no benefit to anyone. The quotation, 'I live; yet not I, but Christ liveth in me,'[9] sounds beautiful, but actually, if we have not arrived at some understanding of what the Christ is, how can we know what it is that is living in us? To the metaphysician, the Christ does not mean what It means to most people in the world today —a man who lived two thousand years ago. The Christ means the Spirit of God in man, the Spirit that animated Christ Jesus, and the mind that animates us.

The term *the Christ* registered very deeply with me early in my spiritual journey, and from that day to this, it has been the guiding light in my life. And why? Because I do not associate it with a man named Jesus but with God Itself, the universal Consciousness or Soul, an individual Presence and feeling within. This has made the Christ so real to me that when I go into the silence and realize, 'I live; yet not I, but Christ liveth in me', there is a depth of understanding that goes with those words, an understanding of what Jesus meant when he said, 'I can of mine own self do nothing'[10] . . . The Father that dwelleth in me, He doeth the works'.[11] Jesus was saying that he was that I AM, that living Christ-presence.

Merely to repeat these words of Jesus is meaningless. Too many people are walking up and down this earth making affirmations and repeating quotations, and nothing happens. Statements are of very little help; they will do nothing for us. It is the conscious realization of the presence of God that does the work; it is coming to that place where we can feel that Christ within, and when we feel that, we have achieved the consciousness of the presence of God.

Then the healing Influence is present—that which goes be-

[9] Galatians 2:20.   [10] John 5:30.   [11] John 14:10.

fore us to 'make the crooked places straight,'[12] that which walks beside us and behind us as our guide and our protection. Thus we carry with us our own healing Influence, and all who meet us during the day feel the Christliness of our presence. This has nothing to do with us as persons; it has nothing to do with the fact that we are good human beings. It has to do with the fact that Christ sits on the throne of our consciousness.

Our consciousness is open to the Christ, and the divine Presence is felt when we have attained this conscious awareness. Throughout the day, we should take as many periods for this realization as our time or work will permit, always being patient and letting that silent Influence come upon us, because it is this healing Influence which renews, restores, and regenerates us and all who come in contact with us. That silence which we have achieved through these short periods of meditation—*that silence* becomes the healing Christ in our consciousness, and that does the healing work.

These frequent periods of silence will make this unfolding consciousness of the presence of the Christ a continuing experience, and the ensuing realization will be one of harmony and peace. Outwardly, it will appear as if we have had a healing of some physical, mental, moral, or financial discord, but we know that what has happened is that the Christ has flooded our consciousness and shown us that there is no sin, disease, lack, or limitation.

'Thou wilt keep him in perfect peace, whose mind is stayed on thee.' [13] The mind must be stayed on God, not on the problem, and we must not permit ourselves to think about the problem a single minute of the day. Instead, let us keep our mind 'stayed on God':

God, the divine Intelligence of this universe, is the Intelligence of all mankind, whether appearing as man, woman, child, animal, or plant. God, the divine Soul of this universe, is the Soul of all mankind.

God, the Spirit, is the substance of all form. There are no material forms or formations: Everything that has form has a

[12] Isaiah 45:2.   [13] Isaiah 26:3.

spiritual form, and God is the substance of that form. Any appearance contrary to spiritual form is illusion.

God is the mind of every individual. Anyone appearing to have a mind apart from God, anyone even claiming to have a mind of his own, is only a temptation coming to me to accept a mind apart from God.

Keeping our mind stayed on God will prevent us from falling into temptation because whenever we see any sign of sin, disease, or mental illness, we shall realize immediately that this is a temptation coming to us to believe that man has a life or a mind apart from God.

God is the mind of this universe, and of all men; God is the Soul of every individual; God is the eternal life of every man, woman, and child in heaven and on earth. God is the life of every individual who has ever lived on earth, is living now, or ever will live. God is the universal life of all being; therefore, there is no diseased life and no dead life.

All life is eternal, immortal, and omnipresent to those of spiritual vision, and those of spiritual vision are those who have come into the agreement that God is the Spirit, the substance of all form—God is the substance of all formation and the law of all formation.

CHAPTER III

ESSENTIALS OF HEALING

THERE cannot be the presence of God AND the absence of any quality of God, or the presence of any quality that is not of God. Anything unlike God is only an appearance or a suggestion of a selfhood or activity separate and apart from God. For example, if we see any evidence of error—drunkenness, immorality, accident, sin, or disease—let us translate that immediately into the word *suggestion* or the word *appearance*. If we do this, we will have taken a big step forward because, whatever the appearance, it does not exist as an actual condition, it does not exist as a thing or a person. It exists only as a false appearance, and when we recognize it as that, it disappears. We have thereby seen through it and destroyed it because its only reality lay in our believing it to be something or someone.

Whenever, then, error presents itself to us as some person or some thing, if we are quick and alert and realize that it is neither a thing nor a person, that it is nothing but a suggestion of a selfhood apart from God, an illusory picture, so quickly will it be met that the sick person will jump to his feet and the drunken one will become sober.

When a call for help comes, just to recognize that this is neither a person, a thing, nor a condition, but only a suggestion, which I am not going to accept, ends it. It is in this immediate recognition that instantaneous healings come. An instantaneous healing will not take place if the practitioner first looks upon the problem as a person, thing, or condition. The only way the illusion can be dispelled is to recognize instantly that we are dealing with appearance or suggestion.

When we look at the streetcar tracks in the distance and see them converging, that is not a condition, and nobody has to pray or give a treatment. All we are called upon to do is to recognize that this is only an appearance. So also, the sky does not sit on the mountain. This exists not as an actual condition to be met, but only as a suggestion coming to the one who is seeing it for acceptance. And what of the mirage? There has never been a mirage that has created wet sands on the desert: no mirage-city has ever been built or torn down. They exist only as appearances, as illusory sense, as suggestions of conditions apart from the normal sense of things.

These examples show what is really meant by the term *mortal mind*, a term which has had widespread usage. The only difficulty is that instead of indicating the nothingness of what we seem to see all around us, it has frightened people into believing they have something to get rid of. To most people who use the term *mortal mind*, it undoubtedly means some evil mind or some mind other than God, some presence or power other than God. But that is not the correct meaning of mortal mind. Originally, it meant the sum total of all human beliefs.

There is only one mind, and that mind is the instrument of God. Where, then, and how does the term *mortal mind* fit into the allness of God? This thing that has been called mortal mind is not an opposite of the mind which is the instrument of God because that mind, being infinite, cannot have an opposite, and thus this so-called mortal mind can be only suppositional. It would be wise for those who can do so to remove that term from their thinking and substitute for it the idea that error in any and every form is only an appearance or suggestion because, if they are convinced that error is only appearance or suggestion, they know they do not have to reach out to do something to it.

That leads us up to the most important part of the teaching of The Infinite Way: Healing work has nothing to do with healing anyone of disease, sin, fear, lack, or limitation: *It has to do with our not accepting a false appearance as reality*. If we accept the appearance or suggestion of error, then we are no different from those who believe that error exists, and we cannot help ourselves or anyone else because we will be the blind leading the blind.

The only difference between a patient and a practitioner is that the patient believes momentarily that this suggestion or appearance exists as an actual condition, whereas the practitioner has come to see that what is appearing as sin, disease, or lack is nothing more or less than illusion. He treats it that way and quickly drops it.

The fullness of God is present as each and every individual. Every person is the absolute allness of God individualized—just as every number 1 is the allness of 1, and every number 2 is the allness of 2. True, appearances testify otherwise. Here is a male and here is a female; here is a person of advanced years, here is one of immaturity, and here is a child. Again appearance! It is not true. Every individual, at whatever stage of his experience, is the fullness and the allness of God. 'Son . . . all that I have is thine'[1]—all that I, God, have is thine. 'Lo I am with you alway.'[2] The fullness of the I is with us, and any evidence to the contrary is only an appearance, an illusion, a false sense. Therefore, every time we come face to face with an individual who will not accept any limiting appearance about us, we must have some measure of healing.

The realization that we ourselves are the fullness of God—that realization on our part or on the part of an illumined consciousness—is the oneness with God that produces healing. Behind this is the truth that God is all and the truth that God, the infinite One, appears as you and as me, and as the dog, the cat, or as the bird. But it is still the One. You are that One; I am that One. You are the fulfilment of that One. This may sound as if I were giving a treatment, but only because every statement of truth is a treatment to any false appearance. However, I am not making these statements in the sense of giving a treatment, but in the sense of presenting the truth of Being because God, whether appearing as one person or as another, has no need of healing. You are that God *appearing*; you are that life eternal; I am that God *appearing*; I am that life eternal—and that is true of every one of us.

Many of our problems stem from the fact that we have been educated into accepting the belief that we are finite, human

[1] Luke 15:31.   [2] Matthew 28:20.

beings, and so we are always seeking some good. One person seeks health, one companionship, one supply, and one a home; and therein lies the error, the reason for delayed or slow healings as well as for failures in the healing work. If all those who today call themselves patients would acknowledge that they are not going to a teacher or practitioner for healing but rather for the revelation of their own completeness, they would hasten the day of their healing.

We are really God fulfilling Itself as individual being. The allness of God permeates us, not for our own sakes, but that we may be the light of the world to the world—to our friends, families, neighbours, and to all those who have not yet come into the light of this truth. You and I are travelling this spiritual path to be a light so that others may see by our example the fruitage of spiritual living—not primarily so that you or I may benefit.

In the scheme of God, it is unimportant whether we ride the wave of prosperity or not. The only possible reason that God could have in prospering any of us is so that others may see the benefits of the spiritual path and reach out for it. So, too, there is only one reason why we should show forth health, and it is not so that we can have a more peaceful mind or a less painful body. It is only so that others will see the fruit of the Spirit and thus be led to follow that way.

It would be a very simple thing for all of us to be healthier and wealthier than we are if we could agree from this point on to stop trying to demonstrate health and wealth for ourselves. If we could give up the attempt to be healed or enriched today, we would come naturally into the grace of God. Our very efforts to heal and to be healed are the stumbling blocks in our pathway. The more a practitioner struggles with a case, the less likelihood there is of bringing out a healing. Healing is not a matter of labour but of love and of Grace. Health, wealth, and harmony—all these come by the grace of God. No one has to work for them, pray, or be deserving of them. All of this comes as the grace of God, and that Grace is made manifest in proportion as we stop thinking of ourselves and our problems and begin thinking of God and thinking out to the world.

Here is one good way to make a beginning: When we go to a practitioner for help, usually we think of ourselves as human beings. Even if we think of ourselves in a spiritual sense, it is most likely as something less than God Itself, as *effect*. Now let us reverse that and think of ourselves as *cause*, as the causative principle of life, as the law unto our being, the law unto our body, the law unto our business. My authority for that? I come well authorized: My authorization is found in the whole teaching of Jesus Christ; it comprises the Gospel according to John; 'I am the way, the truth, and the life[3] . . . I am the resurrection, and the life[4] . . . Have I been so long time with you, and yet hast thou not known me, Philip? he that hath seen me hath seen the Father[5] . . . I and my Father are one.'[6] As we give these truths an opportunity to work in our consciousness, they will bear spiritual fruit and free us from fear.

We cannot be healed of fear while we believe that there is a law outside us—even if we think it is a law of God, because how can we know if we are going to make a connection with that law? Maybe we will fail! But if we are the law of God, how can we escape from ourselves? 'If I make my bed in hell, behold, thou art there.'[7] Yes, if I am in hell then God is there, too, because God and I are one. Let us remember that, and see if we can ever again fear after we have recognized ourselves to be the law, to be the life, the mind, and the Soul of God—all one.

Wherever we go—to a library, to a church or to a movie, a restaurant or even a cocktail bar—let us never believe that the atmosphere in which we live, move, and have our being is dependent on where we are. If we remember this, we shall never be any place, even in a cocktail bar, except to bless, for we will have no other business there. *We carry our own atmosphere with us.* We are the law of God, and wherever we go, the law of God, the presence of God, goes with us. Whether in a cocktail bar, a hotel, a prison, or an asylum, through our

[3] John 14:6. [4] John 11:25. [5] John 14:9.
[6] John 10:30. [7] Psalm 139:8.

C

realization of God as our Life and Soul, we carry the atmosphere of health and wealth with us, and everyone who touches
our consciousness will feel it and be benefited by it:

*I carry the atmosphere of my being with me, and it blesses
not only me, but all who come within range of my consciousness. They must be blessed even if they touch my coat, because
I am permeated with the atmosphere of God.*

*God is my mind, my soul, and the substance of my body,
the law of my body. There is nothing to me but God, and if
anyone sees me as less, he is seeing what his own vision has
created.*

*Here where I am, there is only God; and that is all I see in
anyone.*

The longer we persist in seeing male and female, health and
sickness, wealth and poverty, the longer do we postpone the
day when we realize that we ourselves are the law unto ourselves. Jesus made himself the law unto his own being when
he told Pilate: 'Thou couldest have no power at all against
me, except it were given thee from above.'[8] Jesus knew that
Pilate himself was the law of God, and his knowing that Pilate
was that Law made it impossible for Pilate to kill him—crucify
him, yes, but that was only because he gave his consent to it.
When Jesus gave his consent to the Crucifixion, he probably
wanted to show that even though the human sense of life were
destroyed, he would prove that no one could do anything to
the real life. And he did.

So it is with us. This human world can do anything to us
that we permit it to do. It can crucify us or it can set us free—
but it must have our consent. No one can even die without
giving his consent to death. A person may not openly say, 'I
am ready to die', but he often does say, 'Oh, what's the use?'
or 'I'm giving up', and that is really the consent.

In the same way, no one can be a failure until he gives his
consent to failure. There are certain conditions in the world
that may knock a man down, but if he does not accept failure,

[8] John 19:11.

he will rise above all obstacles and be stronger than ever before. And the reason? Every individual himself is the embodiment of all the God-power there is: You and I are the embodiment of all that God-power. You and I are the law of God that acts upon our business, our body, our family relationships, and as a matter of fact upon the atomic bomb. There is not even an atomic bomb that can destroy us except with our own consent.

If we accept the teaching of Jesus Christ, we lay the foundation for our freedom from this world. I have seen almost every type of disease healed and almost every form of insanity cured. I have seen wondrous and marvellous things in this work, enough to be able to testify that it is a miraculous work, and a person with no other background than yours or mine can do it, just by a little study and the acceptance of a few truths. This is because not only was Jesus the Christ, and Buddha and Shankara also, but you and I are the Christ, as much so as Jesus was, if only we will acknowledge it and claim it.

Within a day, a week, a month, or a year, a dedicated person can do the same kind of healing work that is being done by the best practitioners in the metaphysical world. It is a very simple thing. It comes as a result of knowing first, that we are the very presence of God, and that we need no other law to act upon us for good because we are the embodiment of all the law of good that God has ever given to individual being.

The second thing necessary to know in order to do spiritual healing is that whatever of evil there is, is not reality. It is an appearance or suggestion, and all we have to do is to recognize it as an appearance and let it go. All error is hypnotism! It is enough to know that we are not called upon to heal cancers, tumours, blindness, lack, or limitation, but that all that is necessary is to awaken out of a state of hypnotism. The practitioner must be the dehypnotized person who knows that there is no such thing as an externalized cancer, a tumour, blindness, lack, or limitation. How could there be, if God is the cause or principle of the universe? All that God makes is good.

A practitioner, therefore, is one who knows these two things: (1) All that God is, I am—'Son . . . all that I have is thine',[9] and (2) anything else is an appearance or a suggestion of a selfhood apart from God. His realization is 'Thank you, Father, I do not have to remove disease or heal it. I have only to be dehypnotized enough to know that God is the life and the mind of this individual. I am the law of God in action, and every individual is the law of God in action.'

Begin by reversing your own beliefs about yourself. Reverse the belief that you exist as an *effect* of something, as an image, a reflection, or an idea. You exist as the very presence of God, the allness of God, individually manifest here for the glory of God. Begin now! Instead of looking for some law that is miraculously going to make you healthy, wealthy, and wise, *be that law*. Forget about mortal mind, and see that everything that comes within range of your vision is appearance. Right where the false appearance is, right there, is reality, the universe of God, perfect, entire, complete, and only awaiting your recognition:

'I live; yet not I, but Christ liveth in me.'[10] *All that is real of me is the Christ. Anything else—that which is visible to sense—is but my limited view of the Christ which I am.*

[9] Luke 15:31.
[10] Galatians 2:20.

CHAPTER IV

CONSCIOUS ONENESS

NOTHING is more important in the working out of the problems of human existence than the knowledge of who and what we are, a knowledge that we exist as consciousness, as life eternal. As long as we believe that we are finite and that there is a law of good or a law of evil that can act on, through, or in us, we are likely to believe that in some way we have become separated from good, may become separate and apart from it, or may not find it. The truth is that there is no law of good that can act upon us or that we can contact either through study or prayer.

What we must realize is that we ourselves are constituted of the law of God. We are the law, the mind, and the intelligence of our body, our business, and of our entire universe. If there is any discord or inharmony, it is because we have recognized some power apart from God or acknowledged ourselves to be other than God-being. Probably the most important part of all spiritual revelation is the nature of our true being, because unless we can see that we exist as consciousness, we will always be seeking something, someone, or some law to act upon us, or through us.

'I am the way, the truth, and the life.'[1] This, of course, does not refer to what ordinarily appears to us as humanhood. No human being is God, or even the Christ. But God is the intelligence and the law that constitutes us. What we behold out here as a human being is but our mistaken or false concept of the real you and the real me. It would certainly be sacrilegious to say, of a person who is stupid, dishonest, or deformed, 'You are God'. Nevertheless, God is the sum total of every person—

[1] John 14:6.

whatever his condition—and all that appears contrary to God is the illusion, a false sense or suggestion.

When we are working in the realm of spiritual unfoldment, we do not begin with a human being and go up to God. We begin with God and come forward to that which is the individualization of God, that which is never visible to the human eye. You are consciousness, and all of you that is apparent to me, to my physical senses of sight, hearing, taste, touch, and smell represents my distorted view of you. Therefore, the only way I can ever really know you is through spiritual consciousness.

That is the real sense of communion, and that is where healing takes place—not in calling a person either a human being or a divine idea, but in reaching through the appearance to the reality. When through spiritual sense, we have contacted the reality of a person, we find that God is all the reality there is to him. God, the universal Good, is his individual life, mind, and Soul.

Beginning with God then, we come down to Its individualization and find it to be you and me. It is a great temptation, however, to look at people as human beings and find something in them that needs changing, altering, or improving. Oftentimes we become self-righteous when we find someone doing something we think is wrong and piously state, 'I can forgive him.' This is all part of the human picture and will heal nothing. But when we know that every person is the individualization of God, we can then apply the great law of forgiveness which is not sitting in judgment on a person, first finding him to be wrong and then deciding to be magnanimous and forgive him for being wrong. True forgiveness lies in closing our eyes and in going within to the spiritual sense of things, and there touching the reality of that individual and finding that all Reality is God, and that there never has been a sin, a mistake, or anything to overcome.

Even if we could correct the sins and faults of our friends or loved ones—and did—we still would not have accomplished much in a spiritual way. But when we blot out the picture of *all* humanhood, the good as well as the bad, and come close to the centre of being, close to God, we find that sooner or later that friend or relative is no longer the erring individual he seems to be.

In healing work, we have what appears to be a patient, a practitioner, and God. According to the popularly accepted idea, the patient goes to a practitioner, and the practitioner goes to God, and then God comes down to the patient, and when the circle has been completed we will then have a healing. There is not such a circle; there is no such thing as patient, practitioner, and God, nor is there such a thing as a patient and a practitioner. In reality, there is no patient going to a practitioner and no practitioner reaching out to a patient.

In a great deal of metaphysical practice, there are still attempts made by practitioners to reach the patient's thought because in the early days of this practice that was practically the only known method. Mental practice was then really not so much a matter of mind over matter as mind over mind. There is still literature explaining how the practitioner must work until he overcomes the belief in the patient's mind, and then when the patient's mind is healed, the patient is healed. This is really nothing but suggestion or hypnotism—one mind controlling another and most practitioners have long since outgrown that method. Not only is it not good practice, but often it does not work because it is difficult to send a message from one person to another. The best way is to reach God, and in order to reach God, it is not necessary to send any thought up to God because right here is all there is of both God and man.

If I want to reach God, all I have to reach for is the spiritual centre of my own being, and when I reach that spiritual centre, strangely enough the patient gets the benefit in the form of healing. Through his request for help, the patient has brought himself into oneness with my consciousness, and by holding him in my consciousness, I have brought the patient into this oneness.

It must be remembered that none of this is entirely explainable or comprehensible to the human mind. To illustrate: I have seen innumerable healings of cats, dogs, and birds, and I know that they are much easier to heal than human beings. It is not possible for them to ask for help or even to desire help of a spiritual nature, so how does healing take place? The whole point is this: Everything that comes within range of my consciousness is a part of my universe and, therefore, takes on the atmosphere or complexion of my consciousness. It is not necessary to send out thoughts. In fact, I have never been guilty of sending a thought out to any individual, nor have I ever followed the practice of 'holding a thought' for anyone or about anyone. But when a person asks me for help, he becomes one with the infinite spiritual Consciousness which I am and with Its healing activity.

Inasmuch as I am not interested in making any person a better or healthier *human being*, but only in bringing him into the divine Reality of his own being which is God, I pay no attention to him as a human being. Only in the sacred and secret recesses of consciousness, in communion with God, do all those with any degree of receptivity who are a part of my consciousness come into that outflow of God. Sometimes the patient says, 'I got your thought'. He did not! What he received was not my thought but an impartation from God Itself in the centre of his being because the God at the centre of his being is the God at the centre of my being, and so it is not necessary to reach out to a patient or to find him out in space. Whether he is in the room with me or six thousand miles away, the spiritual Essence of him is right where I am, right within my own Soul-consciousness. Right at the centre of his being, God is; and as God is all there is to me, that is where I am and that is where he is.

My oneness with God constitutes my oneness with every spiritual idea. That is why I am never separate or apart from my spiritual good, whether health, wealth, successful activity, co-operation, students, dollars, a home, or transportation. Regardless of what form these spiritual ideas appear as humanly, I am one with them, not because I am one with all the people of the world, but because I am one with God which spiritually is the embodiment of all.

We can never be without companionship, friends, relatives, transportation, or lodging. We can never be incomplete in any way once we have realized that our oneness with God constitutes our oneness with every spiritual idea, and our oneness with the Father makes all that the Father has ours.

But you may ask, 'Why am I not demonstrating this completeness or fulfilment since it has been proved to be true?' It is because neither the statement nor the quotation is enough. The answer lies in realization. There are innumerable people making these very statements, and countless people reading the Bible. In the last twelve months approximately seven million Bibles were sold. Think how many copies of the Bible there are in the world! But these words, these quotations or statements, are not enough. They are not demonstrable until we, ourselves, have realized the truth of them. That is our work as students on the spiritual path, and it makes no difference what path we are following—what teacher or teaching. In the last analysis, we must come to the realization of truth itself.

Truth is true, but its only benefit to us is in proportion to our realization of that truth. Therefore, we set aside periods of sitting by ourselves and pondering these biblical and spiritual truths until we arrive at the moment of realization. But the correct letter of truth must precede the realization, and above all, it must be understood that there is nothing for us to demonstrate or get.

We ourselves are the fulfilment of all that God is. All that God has is ours, but not until we make this contact with the Infinite Invisible within us, not until we come to realize that there is nothing for us to get, to acquire, or to achieve—not even more truth. There is only the *realization* to be attained, and the first realization is: 'The kingdom of God is within me,' and we must learn to find it in the only place where it is—within us.

When I want to help a person, I do not think of him as a human being—as a patient or student, or as a man or woman. I close my eyes and reach God within me, and when I have reached God, I have reached the spiritual Centre of the person's being, and it will awaken and quicken him to the reality of his being. That is what happens in a spiritual treatment—going within to God, to the Centre of my being and of his being, which are one and the same being.

To say that the kingdom of God is within does not mean that God is within our body. Although It is within and without, It cannot be localized. I can go within and reach that Centre of my being which is God from which all good finds outlet, and there, I can touch that God-centre within my own consciousness, and having done that, I have touched the spiritual reality of the patient. That is how all healings of sin and unnatural phases of human existence are brought forth. Much as people would like to be rid of them, they cannot be overcome humanly, and if will-power is used they often return in a stronger form.

When I touch the spiritual reality of Being, It releases all of the Soul-force of a patient, and then all false desires that were present up to that moment are dissolved—not because I am being kind and benevolent and am going to heal him of smoking or drinking, because that is not my objective. But once this refining Spirit takes over, It eliminates everything unlike Itself. Therefore, as I reach the spiritual Centre of an individual's being, he will find that he is not smoking or drinking, and that many of his tastes have been refined. He may not even enjoy the same kind of books or movies, because this beautiful Soul-sense has been released, is lifting him, and is coming out into active being.

It is all there in the centre of our being now. There is no person so depraved or so sinful that he does not have the whole of the Christ at the centre of his being, and if there is the least desire in him to be free, he can be freed, whether or not he asks for it, because involuntarily he is sending out a call for help. Once our spiritual senses are aroused, we can feel these calls and sense that people are reaching out for help even when they do not know it themselves. They are reaching out for God, for spiritual awakening, and by not trying to be a do-gooder and heal them, but by turning within to our own being and touching the God within us, we will touch the God of them and set them free.

No demand that is made on us is ever made on our human understanding, and therefore, we can meet any and every demand by realizing that the demand is not on our human ability. If we were asked for ten thousand dollars this minute, we should not feel that this demand is made on us as human beings. It is made on the Christ of us, as it was on Jesus when he was asked to feed the five thousand. He could not have fed five thousand out of his human possessions, nor could he have healed the multitudes out of his human wisdom or knowledge.

Only the Christ of the individual, this Infinite Invisible, can meet every demand, whether physical, mental, moral, or financial. We should never permit ourselves to say: 'I wish I had enough understanding to help,' because no one will ever have that much understanding; but the Christ, the Reality of us, can meet it here and now. By turning to the God within and realizing, 'All of this God-energy, all of this Christhood, I am,' we shall find that we have freed those who come for help.

For every financial problem, we turn to the Christ within us, and It meets the need. How, heaven alone knows, but heaven does know! All this is a part of impersonalizing good; all this is a part of opening our consciousness to Infinity. And this is done by realizing that Infinity is the reality of us, and that that Infinity which is the centre of our being can meet every demand that can ever be made upon It.

Because realization is necessary, there must be some way that those of us who have not been trained to find that Centre of our being can attain it. And there is a way: the development of a state of receptivity, the development of the listening ear, keeping the ear stretched out a little bit as if we were always waiting for something that is just beyond ear-shot. There is always a way to reserve one little place in our consciousness for a listening attitude, keeping it open all the time while doing housework, at business, or driving a car.

As we develop this listening attitude, we shall find ourselves receiving not only messages by the power of the Christ, but guidance, leading, and direction—first, in the work which we are now doing, making us better business men or better home-makers, and from there, we shall move up on the spiritual scale into those activities which bring a greater measure of spiritual fulfilment.

After we have developed the listening ear or state of receptivity, we will never again make a false step. This is a matter of practice. The trouble is that we become so busy and so involved in human activities that our whole thought is centred on the external world, but after we have touched the Christ, that becomes the smallest part of our world, because, however important we think our daily life is, we shall find that it is not significant when the Christ has taken over.

Every single one of us is a part of God's plan, but very few are fulfilling even one tiny bit of it. Most of us have not as yet found what God's plan is for us, and so, Martha-like, we compensate for this lack by being busy and 'troubled about many things'.[2]

As we progress spiritually, we devote less and less time to working out our own problems, but if, and when, the opportunity presents itself, we work on the problems of as many others as come into our orbit. We must be willing to give help to those who ask for it, to have no hesitancy in giving it, regardless of the urgency or seriousness of the call, remembering that as human beings, we have no power to give it. It is only in the degree that we touch the divinity of our being that our help is effective.

In our periods of quiet, we keep thought centred on the idea that the Father is the causative principle. The Christ of God is our own consciousness, and when we touch that, we touch the Christ of every individual in the world, and more particularly, we touch the Christ of everyone within range of our human experience. Our oneness with God constitutes our oneness with every spiritual idea.

[2] Luke 10:41.

CHAPTER V

CARRIERS OF THE DIVINE MESSAGE

EVERY word that is spoken and every moment of silence are the same thread of continuity of spiritual Consciousness expressing Itself. But while It expresses Itself in words and in thoughts, Its most powerful mode of expression is silence. Our thoughts and words are very weak substitutes for the real teaching, which comes through the silent and still activity of our Soul and is best apprehended in silence.

Truth is not new. It is as ancient as the ancient of days. The Christ has been made manifest throughout all time in various forms and has appeared as many different people. They stalk through our minds, these people of the past, leaving in our minds the impressions of their thoughts and acts, their desires and aims, their hopes and their faith, and ofttimes their accomplishments and failures.

They relive the history of the ages for us, telling and retelling the struggles of mankind, its comedies and its drama. The philosophy and the religion of all eras pass by as in review, and we watch them go from the freedom of inspired thought to their imprisonment in organization and human interpretation.

We follow the flight of the universal Light as it inspires the meditations and prayers of Buddha, Shankara, Jesus, John and Paul; we see Its illumination touch the consciousness of these inspired souls; and again we witness the sad spectacle of this Light being chained by men in personalities. What is this Light men seek to personify? Why does not man push aside the veil covering his eyes that he may behold the impersonal Saviour and Physician?

Purifier of the individual soul and healer of the personal body, glorious Light of all ages—nameless, formless, universal, impersonal—O man, enlarge your vision and behold It here and now. It walks beside you by day and sits by your side at night; on your journey It travels as Guide and Protector; in your work It serves to inspire and direct. Open your consciousness, now, and let this Presence in.

This Light is the impersonal Christ, the *I* that I am. This teaching of the *I*—not only God as *I*, but individual you and me as *I*—is given forth in such expressions as *I am*, *I am I*, or *I am that*. The message is I AM. That *I* is God. That *I* is individual you and individual me. That which appears to our senses as a human being—as the newborn baby or an aged and dying man or woman—is not the *I*. As a matter of fact, that is not you or I. That is our false sense of both God and man, the limited and finite view, the error that has crept into belief and with which we have so identified ourselves that we say, 'I am sick'; 'I am well'; or, 'I am poor or old'. But the truth is that all this time *I Am* is God.

It is all a matter of identification; it is the recognition that *I* is the infinite individuality of all men. In A.D. 800, Shankara, who gave the world one of the greatest and most absolute teachings, realized the *I Am* of his being. But the teaching of the *I* was given in all its purity by the Master Christ Jesus, given in a form not only absolute, but completely identified with our individual existence and daily affairs. Those who glimpsed this teaching earlier than Jesus gave it forth more as an abstract unfoldment or revelation than as a practical, useful way of life, applicable to everyday living. But Jesus really brought it down to earth, made it provide food for the multitudes, made it produce tax money, made it bring sick bodies back to health and dead ones back to life. He gave it to us in a form that not only makes it clear, but also practical.

Had Jesus been referring only to himself when he taught 'I am the way, the truth, and the life',[1] the teaching would again have set up someone to worship, someone separate and apart from our own being. But Jesus never implied or taught that he was separate and apart from the great truth of being which is universal. As a matter of fact, he exemplified Bronson Alcott's

[1] John 14:6.

definition and description of the real teacher: 'The true teacher defends his pupils against his own personal influence. He inspires self-trust. He guides their eyes from himself to the spirit that quickens him.'

When Jesus said, 'My doctrine is not mine, but his that sent me[2] . . . I can of mine own self do nothing . . . If I bear witness of myself, my witness is not true',[3] he was speaking of what appeared to the world as his humanhood, just as any conscientious teacher of this day would caution his followers not to build him up as a personal saviour, but to look to the Christ of their own being. Any truly spiritual teacher must turn all attention from himself, as a person to the universal Christ, the divine Idea or Son of God, which is his own consciousness.

The consciousness of teacher and student are one and the same consciousness, and that Consciousness is God. There is only one Consciousness, and that Consciousness is your consciousness and my consciousness. It is the infinite Consciousness called God, and it is infinite in its individual expression as you and as me. Just as the fullness of number 12 is included in every manifestation of twelve, whether appearing as twelve dollars or twelve apples or twelve acres, so the sum total of God is manifested in what the world sees as individual you and me. Either the Bible is wrong when it states, 'Son, thou art ever with me, and all that I have is thine',[4] or that must be recognized as literal truth. All that the Father is and has is included in what we call infinite Consciousness; all that the Father is and has is included in what we call individual you and me.

There are people on earth today engaged in every type of activity—artists, writers, sculptors, painters, inventors, lawyers, mechanics, and architects—but usually they are working within the framework of human limitation. They do as much as they can do with their limited human capacity, but when they realize that they are the outlet, the place in consciousness as which the allness of God may appear—if only they will let It—that actually they are the sum total of all the qualities and activities of God, they can then do as much as they have hoped or wanted to do. This teaching of Christ Jesus that God is the

---

[2] John 7:16.   [3] John 5:30, 31.   [4] Luke 15:31.

eternal life of our being is a teaching that ultimately we shall and must manifest here.

John tells us that his book of Revelation was dictated to him by Jesus Christ. That means that it was an impartation to him from the Christ, the Christ which he at the moment was translating as the human Jesus. Many people in moments of illumination have experienced the Christ appearing to them in the form of someone they think they can identify as the man Jesus because they are familiar with photographs, paintings, or pictures of some person's concept of Jesus, usually depicted with the features and colouring of a Nordic, and therefore when the Christ appears, they identify It in that form. The fact is that the man Jesus was of the same colouring as the Arabs of today or the ancient Hebrews of his own day, and very few people in their spiritual illumination have seen such a form.

When a Hindu is illumined and feels the divine presence of the Christ with him, he is more than likely to visualize it as the form of the Buddha, of Krishna, or Mother Kali. However, whether this divine Presence appears as a dark-skinned Jesus or a light-skinned Jesus, as a Buddha or a Shankara, actually it is the Christ which in time of heightened consciousness our finite sense presents to us as some form understandable to us at the moment.

Let us remember that the Christ is always within—within you and me. It was in John who beheld the city not made with hands. He saw the real vision of the Christ, and in my opinion John was the only one of the disciples, probably the only person of that period, aside from the Master himself, who caught the full and complete vision of spiritual life, of heaven on earth. One particular point which clearly indicates the degree of his spiritual consciousness is the revelation of his understanding and realization that there is no real power of evil, that heaven and earth are here and that heaven and earth are one—not two.

More than in anyone of whom we have any knowledge, the vision of the kingdom of God was in Jesus who made it clear that the unfoldment of spiritual truth is not truth over error, not good over evil, not God over devil. How different this is from the Old Testament with its teaching that there is a great power that overcomes all other powers, a great power, a great wisdom or intelligence that does away with sin or disease or opposing armies, and which has power to destroy all evil powers. This is not the teaching of Jesus who went much higher and realized that inasmuch as God is Spirit and Spirit is all, there are no lesser powers, and there is no reality to evil.

This is clearly brought out also in Jesus' experience before Pilate when Pilate said: 'Knowest thou not that I have power to crucify thee, and have power to release thee?' to which Jesus answered, 'Thou couldest have no power at all against me, except it were given thee from above.'[5] And what did Jesus say to Peter when he cut off the ear of the servant of the high priest because they were going to take the Master to prison? Put up again thy sword into his place: for all they that take the sword shall perish with the sword.'[6] If we use material power to help us live we shall die by that same material power. If we think for a moment that we are going to live by some human power or some human good, whether in the form of money in the bank, an army at the front, or medicine or surgery, we shall find that ultimately we will also die by that very power in which we have placed our faith.

Unless we find our safety and security in Spirit, in God, we will always be battling error in some form or using one form of error to overcome or destroy another. When the Hebrews were using what they thought was the Lord Jehovah to overcome the armies of the aliens, they were living by the sword—by human power—and ultimately that same power destroyed them. No one will ever benefit by someone else's loss. Ultimately, all mortal, material power fades out.

But when we turn to the Christ we are not turning to a power that will overcome our errors. This power is the only power there is, a power in which there is no error. That is the real secret of the Christ-message.

Paul carried this teaching of Jesus out into a great part of the world, and up to his time, it was believed that the Hebrews

5 John 19:10, 11.   6 Matthew 26:52.

D

were the only people ready for this message and that it was useless to try to give it to anyone else. But Paul had a broader vision. He saw that it could be carried out to the world and given to all who had a receptive consciousness, a readiness which has to do only with individual unfoldment.

The message of the Christ is not reserved for any particular people. The Jew is as able to receive it as the Gentile, the Moslem and the Hindu as the Christian. But whatever the faith, only those with a prepared consciousness can receive it. Even a Christian whose consciousness is not ready for truth cannot fully appreciate it. Accepting the Christ, therefore, becomes not a matter of race or religion but entirely and completely a matter of individual receptivity and consciousness.

When Jesus stated, 'I can of mine own self do nothing,'[7] he saw this great power as the Father within. In Paul's message, 'I live; yet not I, but Christ liveth in me,'[8] which he carried to the far corners of his world, he caught It as the Spirit of God, the Christ in him. Lao-tze caught the vision and called it Tao; Abraham spoke of It as Friend; Jesus referred to It as the Father; Ramakrishna called it Mother Kali; Paul referred to It as the Christ within—the name or term used means nothing and is of no importance. What is important is the ability to catch the sense or feeling of an inner Presence, an inner Power, something higher than mere humanhood, an awareness, a light or a glow within. Then it makes no difference what name is given It or whether It is seen as personal or impersonal. It is It.

All through the ages, men have appeared and re-appeared with some measure of this Christ. All have not seen It in Its fullness, but nearly all have seen some degree of it. It is abroad in the world today, but again It is abroad only in the measure of the understanding of the individual who is presenting It. As yet there is perhaps no full and complete revelation or unfoldment of It, but this mystical message of oneness, of the one power, runs through many of the modern teachings and writings. Most important of all, we have been born into an age where the mystical teachings are reaching the highest level ever before known except probably during the time of the

---

[7] John 5:30.   [8] Galatians 2:20.

Master and of John. In their day, it was most likely experienced by them alone, but in this age, it is possible for you and me as well as many others to attain heights of understanding and demonstration never before known, except in the isolated cases of the spiritual giants of all ages.

That is because in this century, for the very first time, the nature of error is being made known to the world at large. In this era, we are learning that error is not real, not something to be overcome or destroyed, but is pure illusion, belief, or suggestion which has been built up in human consciousness. If error in the form of sin or disease existed as reality, we would be in the position of looking for a God to overcome some power of evil, for a truth with which to fight error, for a God to do battle with the devil. In the degree that we do that, we are living according to the Old Testament and are back in the Judaic age. But we are not on the path of destroying error: We are on the path of knowing that it does not exist as a reality. The examples of the mirage on the desert, the sky sitting on the mountain, the tracks coming together, the snake in the rope show not that a great Power—a God—is needed to correct or destroy these, but that they have no real existence.

Those of us who understand this principle no longer look for a cause for disease because we know that *in a spiritual universe* disease has no existence, no reality, and no power. The non-power of disease is evidenced by the many dedicated spiritual healers who, contrary to medical belief, fail to contract the infections and contagions to which they are exposed in the course of their practice. What we have to do is to come into the actual consciousness of the nothingness of what appears as sin and disease so that we no longer criticize, judge, or condemn those who at this moment seem to be indulging in it or are victims of it, but rather we stand back and smile, knowing the unreality of all error and the ultimate freedom of even those who at this moment appear to be enmeshed in it.

Before coming into a spiritual teaching, we may have turned to the man Jesus and looked to him for our help, or if we were of other faiths, we may have looked to a God up in the sky. But from the moment of our entering the world of Spirit, we look to no person. We look now to the impersonal Christ—the Father within—the Christ that liveth in us. Even though we may turn to someone for temporary help, we do not believe that the mind or consciousness through which he speaks is other than our own. We do not accept the belief that the power that brings our healing comes from any truth other than our own consciousness.

If we look upon the consciousness of our teacher as other than our own, we are cheating ourselves of entrance into heaven. Heaven, or harmony, is divine, but it is our own consciousness, and it is within our own consciousness that heaven is found. The way to heaven is the way to the centre of consciousness. Let us never forget that, and let us never transfer power to a practitioner or teacher, even when we appeal to him for help. Instead, let us remember that the help ultimately is coming from within our own consciousness, even if it is the practitioner or teacher who momentarily calls it forth.

The Master said, 'If I go not away, the Comforter will not come unto you.'[9] So it is that sooner or later some practitioner or teacher will have to say to every patient or student who relies on him, 'If I do not go out of your life, you will look to me forever, and you must find this thing in your own consciousness.' Those practitioners and teachers, who today are turning students and patients more and more to the consciousness of their own being, to an absolute and utter reliance on the Christ of their being, are truly showing them the way to heaven.

[9] John 16:7.

CHAPTER VI

BE A BEHOLDER

WE were not born into this world just to do healing work, any more than Jesus came to earth to cure people's ills or raise them from the dead. Lazarus, even though raised from the dead, passed on some time later and probably only a change in the date on his tombstone was involved. The more clearly we can perceive the unreal nature of any form of error and understand that what appears to us as error in any form is not error at all, that there is not really either a sin or a disease that has to be overcome, but that both sin and disease exist only as illusory experience or mental beliefs, the closer we shall come to being free of them and attaining spiritual consciousness, which is of course far more important than the healing work which we are doing in this age and at this period of our unfoldment.

It was in 1928 that I lost all desire for the things of the earth in the sense of their having any attraction for me or making any demands upon me. Good music, good friends, good books, and good food still give me pleasure, but these are no longer a necessary part of my experience. I have learned to be in the world but not of it, to enjoy the good things of this world, but not to miss them when they are not a part of my experience. I have become aware of something in people with which I can commune and tabernacle. It makes no difference what their educational, financial, or social background is. I can enjoy mental or spiritual companionship with them. There is nothing of any nature they have that I desire or want or would go out of my way to get. I cannot be too happy when they are with me or too sad when they are away from me. We are just good friends at all times because I have touched a place in their consciousness which makes this possible, and therefore I know them more or less as they really are.

I can love everyone on this earth. In fact, I had a very hard time hating Adolph Hitler—it was not easy for me to hold harsh feelings even toward him. There is something I have seen in men and women that is beautiful, although outwardly they may not be manifesting it at the time, but undoubtedly some of those individuals who are not manifesting it today, sooner or later will show forth what spiritual discernment enabled me to see even when it was not in evidence. Imagine a world of such relationships!

And that is the only way we can end war. Let us not think for a minute that treaties will end war or that disarmament will. When war came in 1939, Britain was unprepared, but that did not prevent war. Nothing of a human nature will prevent war. Regardless of how public-spirited the citizenry may be or how competent, trustworthy, and upright the heads of governments, tomorrow there may be scoundrels in their places who can overthrow in one generation all the good that has been built up over many years.

Peace, therefore, must first be established in individual consciousness before it can become a collective experience; and that individual peace will come only when each individual realizes his oneness with God and recognizes that all the good he is to receive must be received from God, not from a person.

Whatever good we receive will come from God—the good of our consciousness which we are always attracting, but until we can receive it directly, we shall have to receive it through some human avenue.

My supply comes to me directly from my own consciousness. No one is responsible for it. Today, however, you may be the avenue through which it comes to me; you may be that point of consciousness receiving good through me, and thereby I receive my good through you—*but not from you*. The infinite consciousness which I am will provide my supply for me, and as long as it is necessary to have an avenue or channel, that avenue or channel will be provided. The same is true of you.

When we realize that all our good flows from our own consciousness, we can no longer be envious or jealous of another's possessions, have a desire for them, or even a mild wish for them, because we can have all we need and want by opening our consciousness and letting it flow out. When you and I individually come to the place where you have nothing that I desire, and I have nothing that you desire, where we feel that the infinity of good is flowing from our individual consciousness—that Consciousness which we call God—then we shall see how little strife there will be. And there is no other way. Only through an illumined spiritual consciousness, one which knows that the place whereon he stands is holy ground, can this be brought about. Why is it true that the place whereon we stand is holy ground? Because 'I and my Father are one,'[1] and wherever I am, God is. We are not two. We cannot become separated from one another.

'If I make my bed in hell, behold, thou art there'[2] in the sickroom, the prison, the asylum, the poorhouse.

If only we can realize God as our individual being, we shall very quickly experience a change of consciousness that will attract to us all the good, not only what is necessary for our development, but an abundance of it for our joy.

'I am come that they might have life, and that they might have it more abundantly.'[3] The *I* within us is come not merely to supply our needs, but that we might have life and life more abundantly—health and wealth without measure. There is no limit to the amount of health and wealth we may have under spiritual law, but always there must be that spiritual illumination. In this healing activity, our purpose is not to make human beings healthy or wealthy, but to bring spiritual illumination to them, and then these other things will be added unto them. That is the Messianic promise. 'Seek ye first the kingdom of God and his righteousness; and all these things shall be added unto you.'[4]

When the essence and substance of two particular passages from the Bible, which are an important part of the unfoldment of the message of The Infinite Way, become part of your own consciousness and you really understand them, they will begin to live for you and function for you eternally. It is not

[1] John 10:30.
[2] Psalm 139:8.
[3] John 10:10.
[4] Matthew 6:33.

from memorizing and reciting these words that any permanent benefit will be derived. It is only as these inspired passages become part and parcel of your being that they can transform your experience.

The first of these passages is Luke 12: 22-32:

Take no thought for your life, what ye shall eat; neither for the body, what ye shall put on.

The life is more than meat, and the body is more than raiment.

Consider the ravens: for they neither sow nor reap; which neither have storehouse nor barn; and God feedeth them: how much more are ye better than the fowls?

And which of you with taking thought can add to his stature one cubit?

If ye then be not able to do that thing which is least, why take ye thought for the rest?

Consider the lilies how they grow: they toil not, they spin not; and yet I say unto you, that Solomon in all his glory was not arrayed like one of these.

If then God so clothe the grass, which is today in the field, and tomorrow is cast into the oven; how much more will he clothe you, O ye of little faith?

And seek not ye what ye shall eat, or what ye shall drink, neither be ye of doubtful mind.

For all these things do the nations of the world seek after: and your Father knoweth that ye have need of these things.

But rather seek ye the kingdom of God; and all these things shall be added unto you.

Fear not, little flock; for it is your Father's good pleasure to give you the kingdom.

Throughout all my writings, I emphasize as the vital part of individual unfoldment: *Take no thought*. That does not mean to become lazy mentally or to sit back and wait for some mysterious God to come and work for you. The take-no-thought attitude is not one of mental indolence or blind faith. In fact, it is the very opposite of laziness. It is one of mental alertness and spiritual expectancy.

When we are living in the constant realization that God is our very own consciousness, and that this consciousness which we are knows our need and is forever fulfilling it, we cannot become lazy and sit back and call for an unknown God to do something for us. Neither can we just go about our human business and expect that all good will flow in. Rather must we learn to live in a state of spiritual expectancy and alertness, with an ear open spiritually as if a divine message were waiting to come in and we always at the standpoint of waiting to hear it.

The second important passage is Zechariah 4:6:

Not by might, nor by power, but by my spirit, saith the Lord of Hosts.

This is not an invitation to become mentally lazy or to sit around waiting for good to happen. It says, 'Not by might!' It is not the physical or mental effort that we make. It is spiritual awareness. It is the realization of a spiritual power functioning in us and through us and as us that does the work. Making the transition from living humanly to living spiritually requires that the central theme in our consciousness at all times be God.

When we are advised to take no thought for our life, it does not mean that we do not think. We think, but we do not think about the things we need. We think about God, and the more we realize God as the mind and Soul and Spirit of our being, the more we are really thinking correctly about God and keeping our mind stayed on Him.

God is not a God afar off. He is nearer than hands and feet, closer than breathing. Right where I am—sitting, standing, walking, or talking—there God is unfolding and expressing Itself as my being and my affairs.

'But seek ye first the kingdom of God, and his righteousness;

and all these things shall be added unto you.'[5] When we seek the consciousness of the presence of God, all things will be added unto us. This is being a beholder. Heretofore, we may have been hard workers, depending on good, hard physical labour to accomplish our objective. Maybe we prided ourselves on being faithful and conscientious workers in a human way. And perhaps, as we came into metaphysics, we become faithful mental workers and gave ourselves, our families, and our friends good mental treatments. All those things were stepping stones to this. From now on, however, we are not going to use physical or mental work as the springboard for our good. Now we will let our good unfold through, and as, our spiritual consciousness.

Be a beholder! Watch, as if you were looking over your shoulder, to see what God is bringing to pass in your experience —*the God that is right where you are*. Watch everything that you do, everything that you hear, everything that you think. The God that sits at the centre of your consciousness knows all that is going on. And you are watching God appear as form, watching God unfold as your experience. God is not something separate from the form in, and as which, God appears. *God is the substance and essence of that form.*

God does not send supply: God appears *as* supply. God is not only your supplier, God is your supply. And if at this moment you see God as food on the table, that is merely your interpretation of God *appearing*. Let us call that one of the added things. Actually, God is unfolding as our supply, and there is no separation or division between God and our good.

This concept of *God appearing as* is very important because now, as we watch our lives unfolding, we will not see a group of human beings coming into our experience, or a certain amount of dollars. We shall be seeing God appearing in infinite form and variety—no matter what form It appears as. It might be a vacation trip, a new teaching, an unfoldment within our own consciousness, or it might be the height of spiritual illumination. Whatever the form, it will be God appearing to us directly. We may see it in the form of Jesus

[5] Matthew 6:33.

Christ, or our mother or father. Nevertheless, it will be God appearing to us in a form that we can understand, and so we never separate God from any of the forms as which God appears.

Being infinite, God appears in, and as, infinite forms and variety. God has not always appeared in the same form to us and, because of the infinity of God, may never appear twice the same. Infinity will never end. Life will never end. Life cannot end at a hundred years, for Life, being infinite, must appear in infinite form and variety continuously and endlessly.

Body is one of the infinite forms as which God, and divine Substance and Essence of the universe, is appearing. The body cannot decay or decompose unless we accept the universal belief that we have a material body which functions in time or space. God is the essence and substance of you and me *as* flesh and blood and bone. The flesh, the blood, and the bone are only our translation or interpretation of the divine Spirit appearing as all Its forms. There is no such thing as God *and* your body and my body. It is God appearing as body. It is the same substance and spirit that our consciousness is made of, only in another one of Its infinite forms and varieties.

Look at a table. There is not table *and* wood there. You cannot separate wood from table. The wood is appearing *as* the table. There is no such thing as you and your body or as me and my body :

'I and my Father are one.'[6] I and my body are one. My body will never die—it never will! It never will age or decompose. My state of consciousness is always held to God, always held to the spirit of Truth, and is forming me every single day. And because there is no time, it will go on doing that forever.

Nothing is appearing to you except God in infinite form and variety. Therefore, God is appearing to you as body. At this moment you may be entertaining a material concept of your body, but you must change that. Your body is spiritual, formed

[6] John 10:30.

of the substance of God, or Consciousness, and if you want to change your body, you must change your concept of body, and then your body will respond because your body is the product of your consciousness.

Beauty likewise must appear in infinite forms and varieties. One flower, for example, is not more beautiful than another, and it is only because we do not all appreciate the same form of beauty that some of us prefer one to another, but beauty can appear as a rose, a daisy, or as a sunflower.

Although we do not really identify spiritual experience with human needs in the sense of the specifics of trying to demonstrate a place to live or trying to demonstrate an automobile, which would be taking thought for things, yet there is a connection. As we become conscious of God appearing to us in infinite forms and varieties, It will always appear in the form necessary to our understanding at the particular moment. If our need is a house in which to live, an automobile, or a seat on a railroad train, it will appear to us in that form. It will be God appearing, but it will be translated into the necessary form of the moment.

Never must we dishonour God by turning to God for improvement, employment, or a home. We do, however, turn to God for the consciousness of the presence of God appearing as any and every form, and if our need happens to be a needle and thread or transportation on a jet plane, God must appear as that form. But let us demonstrate it through the conscious awareness of the presence of God in every form.

Take no thought for your life, what ye shall eat; neither for the body, what ye shall put on.

Your Father knowest that ye have need of these things . . . for it is your Father's good pleasure to give you the kingdom.

Luke 12:22, 30, 32.

This is a principle; this is a law; and we either fulfil the law or we do not demonstrate it. The law is that we must not try to demonstrate person, place, or thing, but *Grace*. So if God has not appeared as our need, it is because we have been violating this Messianic teaching, trying to get things and persons and places. How then can we come into the promise? We must first seek the kingdom of God and his righteousness and resolve to take no thought for these other things. Our heavenly Father, which is our divine consciousness, never further away than our own breathing, knows our needs and supplies them. By might? By struggle? No, by my Spirit—by the natural flow.

And here let no one misunderstand me; let no one say that I teach that we do not have to do anything. This I do not believe, for I myself am a hard worker. I work twenty-one hours out of every twenty-four—day and night. But I am not working *for* anything. I am doing the work that is given me to do this minute. Under this Messianic promise, I cannot be lazy, and I do not believe that Jesus was lazy. The Spirit goads us on, and although it gives us rest, never can we be lazy.

"Not by might, nor by power, but by my spirit"[7] does not mean that we should move out to the country and let God do it. It means that instead of being concerned for the things of the world, we must be concerned with the things of God and do what is given us to do, and do it to the best way we know how to do it. And so, even though we are cautioned to take no thought, when a call comes for us to do something, let us be alert and do it, not because we are responsible for the result, not because our human activity is of itself important, but because our human activity is merely carrying out the divine command on our level of consciousness .

If we are not fulfilling every obligation and living up to our own highest sense of right, then somewhere we are failing in our spiritual understanding. When Jesus said, 'Who is my mother? and who are my brethren?'[8] it was not that he was a negligent son or brother. He was bringing out the truth that his greatest responsibility was to those who were seeking the spiritual path of God, and that nothing must interfere with that. That done, he could go back and be a son—and he would want to be a good one.

We must never allow our human or family obligations to interfere with our spiritual unfoldment or growth. This does

[7] Zechariah 4:6.   [8] Matthew 12:48.

not mean ignoring or neglecting these obligations, but it does mean that we will have to see that our families are cared for in whatever way best suits their particular needs while at the same time we are enabled to carry on our spiritual interests and activities without obstruction or interference.

The man who wanted to find 'the pearl of great price'[9] was told to sell everything he had in order to obtain that pearl, and whether or not you are aware of it, let me assure you that no sacrifice of material comfort or welfare is too much to pay for that pearl.

Undoubtedly, spiritual development is pounding away at your consciousness, or you would not be reading this book. Something of a spiritual nature is trying to break through and will not let you rest until you have attained your goal, so even if you have to sacrifice some material good at this moment in order to achieve that spiritual unfoldment, do not shrink from these sacrifices. Rather, be prepared for them because you may have to sacrifice much to attain this spiritual development, but it will be well worth every sacrifice, for when you have achieved even a measure of it you will find that you have everything else you need in the world.

I know that there are many people who believe that they should be able to keep all the material comforts of life and attain their spirituality as well. It will not work. Look at the lives of Jesus, John, and Paul—of anyone who has ever attained spirituality—and note how little interest they had in material living.

Living the spiritual life will not deprive you of normal living even though it may temporarily interfere with your normal routine. But it is worthwhile ! It is a new kingdom. It does not take you away from people. Rather do you learn to find the spiritual centre in everyone and then you have something in common with all.

To the Ten Commandments, Jesus could only add, 'Thou shalt love thy neighbour as thyself.'[10] This we could not do, if that love had anything to do with physicality, with educational, social, or financial background. Those are the barriers that

[9] Matthew 13:6.   [10] Matthew 19:19.

separate us from one another. It is only as we meet all on a spiritual level that we can see *through* physicality and materiality that we can look above and beyond any kind of a financial rating found in Dun and Bradstreet, that we can love them—and I mean love !

Be a beholder ! Our attitude is always that of sitting as if at a movie and watching the picture unfold. The entire movie is complete on that roll of film, and as we watch it unreel before our eyes, in the back of our mind we know that there is a happy ending already prepared. So we go through all the headaches, heartaches, and grief only to end up with a smile when the lights come on. As beholders, we are in much that same position, because God is unfolding Itself as our life. I know that there is a happy ending even if I have to go through one or two world wars, even if I have to go down to death's door to come to a place where for a few days I do not have enough money to pay for food. But none of that has anything to do with the final result because I know that God is unfolding this plan of my life, and therefore it can result only in a happy ending. So I am not overly concerned with isolated parts of the picture because I can live only one minute at a time.

'Ye are witnesses.'[11] Be a witness ! Be a beholder—a beholder of God's unfoldment as your experience. And as you behold, you will find that you truly have to take no thought. As a matter of fact, there is no way you can take thought. True, you will be thinking, and every minute you will be given something to think about, but learn to be a *beholder*.

Whether in my home or in a hotel room, every morning I begin the day in a state of expectancy, wondering what the Father is going to put on my desk that day. Whatever it is, it will be God appearing, and I take care of it. I have built up this consciousness of knowing always that God is, God unfolding and appearing to me in some form. You can do that same thing. You can attain the attitude of a beholder so that every day when you awaken you say, 'This is God's day. I wonder what pictures He will present to me today.' Begin to

[11] I Thessalonians 2 : 10.

see that it is God who is presenting the pictures to you each and every day.

'Thou shalt have no other gods before me.'[12] In the world of religion, there is a God and a devil. So, too, in the world of philosophy, there is good and evil. And that is where The Infinite Way is different from every religion and every philosophy. It takes the First Commandment literally—only one power. That separates this teaching from every teaching on earth. There is only one power—not just in reality, but *only one power*. With that as our basic principle, we cannot turn around and wonder what evil influences or powers are acting, or are going to act, in our experience. Instead we awaken in the morning with the idea, 'I am going to watch what God unfolds,' and then in everything that occurs we realize it is God unfolding Itself as our experience. Whether the appearance is good or bad, we can wait to see what lesson God wants us to get out of it or in what way we may have missed the direction and how God is pulling us back, always remembering there is no presence or power apart from God.

Awaken in the morning knowing that God is appearing and unfolding *as* your experience. Never deviate. If you receive bad news or have an accident, do not be tempted, do not be double-minded and say, 'This is error'. Nothing but God is appearing, and if it takes a pain to make you re-interpret it, it will have to be that way. Stand on the First Commandment. Acknowledge God—not a lesser power acting upon God's power, but God, the consciousness of your being—as the governing Principle, governing all that is from the movement of the stars and the planets to the growing of a plant.

In the same way, we will not acknowledge that error can do anything to us or wonder why error is doing this or that today. There is no error except what we accept into our own experience. God is the only presence and the only power, and everything that is happening to us today, this minute, is happening as the result of God operating in, and for, and through, and *as* us. 'In all thy ways acknowledge him, and he shall direct thy paths,' and it does not say, 'in all thy *good*

[12] Exodus 20:3.

ways'. It says, 'in all thy ways'.[13] Acknowledge God as the only
Actor in your experience, as the only presence, the only Power,
the only Law, the only Substance, the only Cause, the only
Effect—God, and only God !

Acknowledge the divine infinite Consciousness which is your
consciousness. Acknowledge the infinite eternal Life which is
your life. Acknowledge no life apart from your God-life, and
you will never have the experience of dying. It will never
happen to you if you hold fast to the First Commandment.
God alone is universal life and God is the reality of your being.
Do not separate God from Its forms. God is not sending something to you. *God is appearing to you in infinite form, in infinite variety, and in infinite experience. God is appearing to
you as.*

[13] Proverbs 3 : 6.

E

CHAPTER VII

MAKE LIFE AN ADVENTURE

IF there is no change in our consciousness today, there will be no change in our outer experience tomorrow. In proportion as some change takes place in our consciousness, in that proportion is there an improvement in our outer affairs—either in health, personal relationships, or supply. If we maintain truth actively in consciousness, it would be as impossible for us to be in the same place today that we were a week ago as it would be to toss raisins into bread dough and not have raisin bread.

That which goes into consciousness must come forth as manifestation. That which becomes a part of consciousness as truth must appear as manifestation. There is no such thing as truth *and* manifestation: *Truth itself appears as manifestation.*

Spirit is not something separate and apart from the forms it assumes. Spirit is the *substance*, and the *form* is Its manifestation. Therefore, if truth appears in, or as, our consciousness, if truth appears in, or as, the Spirit of our being, it must also appear as manifested form. All improved states of consciousness must appear as improved experience, but unless we consciously make the *decision* to act and live in a higher way and on a higher level, we are not going to have the manifestation on a higher level.

Just as we have learned not to believe in an evil law or an evil power, so we cannot sit back passively and believe that there is a God or a law that is going to do something good in us, through us, for us, or to us. There is no such thing as a law that acts upon us except as we give it power through our belief in it. We can accept any belief and thereby make it a law unto ourselves. There is no power in the stars to act upon us, but it is possible for us to make a god of anything. We can pick up a piece of metal or a penny and call it a good-luck charm and in the measure of our faith derive some benefit from it, but that is not the law of God, and it is not permanent.

There is no law of evil or of good that can act upon us because we ourselves are the embodiment of all law:

God is the law of the universe, God is the substance of the universe, and my oneness with God makes me a law unto my universe—unto my world. God, the indivisible God, is the individual law unto my being through my own state of consciousness.

Sometimes we see friends or members of our family making serious mistakes—at least, serious in our opinion—and we would like to reach out, help, and prevent them from doing so, but in doing that, we would be guilty of interfering with another person's individual demonstration of his own being. Every one of us ultimately will come into heaven, into the kingdom of God, but we may be going by different routes.

There are some people so constituted that they can make their way to heaven a gradual and beautiful ascent without needing discords to push them forward. Others will not find themselves coming into heaven without troubles to spur them on. Serious diseases, therefore, have often been the means of driving some people to God. Unless they reach the place where the doctor says, 'There is no hope for you', they will not be willing to give up their worldly pursuits and find their way to God. With others, it may be poverty. Whatever it is, the ultimate will be to bring each one of us into heaven.

There are many people who have never found God, many people content and completely satisfied with the human sense of good they are experiencing—good health, good supply, and good human relationships. They believe there is a God, but they have not found Him, and they are, therefore, on the level of good materiality. It is a different story when they find God. Then all phases of human or mortal conditions drop away, and no longer do they have to be told to be better human beings.

Our part now is to realize that God is the law unto our

being, and for that reason we ourselves have it within our power to decide, and must decide, what way we shall go. When we make the decision to follow the spiritual path, we shall find that there are many temptations to lead us away from it, and we have to be very firm in our determination to let nothing interfere with our progress spiritually.

There are many demands made upon us when we take this path. There may be a teacher seven hundred or seven thousand miles from us whom we feel it is imperative to reach, one whom we *have* to find at this particular point along the journey. That calls for time and for money, and it is up to us to make the decision whether we are going to sacrifice some material form of good in order to follow our spiritual leadings. Again, a way must be found to take care of family responsibilities in a generous and loving way without letting them interfere with our spiritual progress. Always something in some way will intrude to impede our progress—*if we let it.*

The Bible points out the value of spiritual teaching when it calls it 'the pearl of great price.'[1] And so, when we find that 'pearl', the particular teaching that says to us, 'This is it; this is the way', then let us work with it until the unfoldment or revelation of God floods our consciousness. When we have touched even the hem of the Robe, we shall no longer need either books or teachers. We shall continue studying, of course, and may attend church occasionally, not because of a need for spiritual enlightenment, but rather because of the joy experienced through the sharing of spiritual views. We read inspirational books and associate with others on the same path, not because we need them, but because there is never a time when we cannot benefit from the exchange of ideas.

We will be *in* the world, even though we will not always be *of* the world. This work is not meant to take anybody out of the world or to make of anybody an ascetic or a hermit. On the contrary, it is meant to make us the *light* of the world, and that light has no right ever to be hidden. The real purpose of all our work is to come into the conscious awareness of the

[1] Matthew 13:46.

presence of God, but that purpose must first be made a point of decision before it can be carried out.

The most important point in gaining that awareness is to acknowledge God to be all there is to us. When we acknowledge God to be our mind, the life of us, the Soul, and the Spirit, when we make the acknowledgment that God is the only element in, and the only activity and law of, our being, then we have taken the most essential step in becoming aware of God.

There is no selfhood apart from God. God is one—infinite and indivisible—appearing as each and every individual. The allness of God appears individually as you and as me. We are not a part of God. We are not a particle of God. It is not like the relationship of a drop of water with the ocean—not at all. You and I are the allness of God! You are the allness of God; I am the allness of God. The allness of God appears individually *as you* and *as me*. It is like the allness of the number 12, appearing in every number 12, whether as pies or grains of sand. Always the entire number contains the total value of 12.

So it is that this totality of God appears as individual you and me. You are *all* the truth, *all* the life, *all* the immortality of God—and so am I. You cannot be more truthful than to be truth. Either you are all of truth or you are not truth. You cannot be *more* life than life itself: You always have existed and always will exist. You cannot be *more* immortal than immortality.

This same principle is true of every facet of God. A person cannot be partly intelligent, and yet be of God: He is the sum total of intelligence. Therefore, God's infinite intelligence is his individual intelligence. The most essential point in becoming aware of God is to make the acknowledgment:

I, of mine own self, am nothing. God is the allness of me, the mind, the life, and the Soul of me. God is the sum total of me; God is the substance of my body—the actual substance of my body.

A second point in becoming aware of God deals with the

subject of sleep and how to arrive at the place of requiring less sleep. That, of course, cannot be made a matter of human will, for to force the issue would be to wreck our human sense of health. It must be a matter of spiritual demonstration, which can be achieved by practice.

In my own case, for many years I have never had more than three or three-and-a-half consecutive hours of sleep out of the twenty-four, and sometimes much less. Yet I have had no sense of needing sleep or of being tired. I have trained myself never to jump into bed at night in a hurry to get some sleep, but instead to sit down for at least three to five minutes before getting into bed and in that period opening my consciousness to God in the sense of 'I and the Father are one; and where I am, there is conscious awareness of that'.

Before going to sleep, everyone on this path should learn to open his consciousness to God, even if only for a few minutes, and under no circumstances should he go to bed without doing this. Then, instead of lying in bed and thinking about the problems of the day or of what must be done tomorrow, he will lie there in the thought of conscious oneness with God, and with this thought fall asleep.

Anyone who follows such a procedure will eventually find that instead of sleeping the whole night through, he will wake up in the middle of the night, and that is when the first really difficult step begins, because when this happens, he must get up out of bed, have something warm to drink, if he likes, but get up, and for several minutes feel that conscious oneness with God. Then, if he wants to go back to bed, he should do so by all means. Through this practice he is gradually filling himself with the presence of God, and by degrees he will overcome the necessity for prolonged periods of that state of unconsciousness we call sleep.

One night, I was awakened out of sleep with this statement: 'Seek ye first the kingdom of God,'[2] and then in big letters, '*and His rightness*'. It was then for the first time in my life that I understood those words. We all know what good human life is—a little extra income, a little extra wisdom, a little extra

[2] Matthew 6:33.

health. But what is His rightness? What is the spiritual sense of health, the spiritual sense of supply, the spiritual sense of good? And there we have the whole secret. Imagine waking up out of a deep sleep and having a lesson like that unfold and appear. Such sleep is not unconsciousness, but merely a resting of the body, because the inner mind is functioning.

That is the place to which we ultimately will come, not merely to a point of staying awake more or less for the greater part of the day and night, but to a point of conscious intelligence, whether awake or asleep, and then it does not make any difference whether we stay in bed two, eight, or ten hours out of the twenty-four. It does not really matter as long as we are consciously functioning, as long as rest is merely a resting of the body. The operation of God can go on while the eyes are closed and we are apparently asleep, but not if we go to sleep in an unconscious state.

When I retire at night, I make the decision that everyone who reaches out to me for help must touch the Christ of his own being and get Its help. It is not my human knowledge, but the divine Consciousness of me with Its Christ which provides the help. And this divine Consciousness never sleeps. When I make the decision not to turn off my contact with those who are looking to me as a practitioner and when I consciously realize that everyone who reaches out to me during the night is reaching out, not to me as a human being, but to the Christ of me and that Christ is awake and healing now, the patient receives his help.

That help comes because of the fact that, even in my sleep, I, the reality of me, am not asleep. My body is at rest; my human thinking is at rest; but the Consciousness of me which is God, the Christ of me which is the individualization of God, is ever awake and ever healing. So let us not look upon this as an attempt to sleep less hours or to be in bed a shorter period of time. The point is to come to the conscious awareness of the Christ, awake or asleep.

To sum this up then, first, before going to bed, we should have two or three minutes of meditation to establish our oneness with God. Then when we get into bed, we should not allow ourselves to think about today's problems or yesterday's problems, but spend that minute before we fall asleep in maintaining our conscious oneness. Then, if we wake up in the middle of the night, we do not try to go back to sleep, but get out of bed for a few minutes and sit in meditation. After that, we may go back to bed, or if we feel like writing or cooking or doing something else, we do that.

Let us not be concerned if we feel more comfortable when we are in bed eight hours out of twenty-four, but let us make our rest a conscious oneness with God, instead of an unconscious sleep, so that it becomes merely a rest while our healing and creative work goes on. Life must now not be lived according to established patterns. Life now becomes an adventure because there is something worth looking forward to rather than just falling into the habit of living twenty-four hours a day in some automatic routine manner.

CHAPTER VIII

TITHING

SOONER or later, we all have to learn the meaning and importance of tithing because this practice carries us to our highest sense of gratitude, and gratitude is one facet of the vast subject of love. Tithing is usually understood to mean that if ten per cent of our income is given to some charitable or spiritual purpose, we will in some mysterious way have pleased God and so will be rewarded. Personally, I think that this teaching is entirely incorrect.

There is no virtue in giving when there is any sense of a future tense connected with it. If our giving, whether in contributions to a charity, a church, or to a teacher, carries with it any thought that we will receive some benefit from it, it is best not to give.

Giving should always be from the standpoint of gratitude for that which already is—health, wealth, happiness, and peace. We cannot *get* health and we cannot *get* wealth, we cannot *get* happiness, we cannot *get* peace. Those things were established from the beginning. They are a part of the divine Consciousness, and they will unfold as our individual consciousness in proportion to our turning within for that unfoldment, and in proportion to our devotion to the spiritual sense of life.

It is perhaps true that many of us are not yet at that point of consciousness where we are able to realize our oneness with God sufficiently to receive a spiritual message without mediation. And yet God needs no mediator. Because of our oneness with God, truth can reveal itself in our consciousness without any person talking to us or without our reading a book; but inasmuch as we have not reached that state of communion and conscious oneness, truth interprets Itself to human consciousness as a book, a church, or a teacher, until the time comes when our conscious oneness with God enables us to accept truth without any human means.

God knows nothing about human teachers or teachings, or human places of worship. If God had made our churches, none of them would ever have been bombed or burned. It is we who create these places of worship because we need them just as we need teachers and books. Let us call all of this the activity of God, and see that the activity of God interprets Itself to us as teachers, churches, or books, and then let us understand that the activity of God acting through us, or as us, may appear as man, woman, or book, but it comes to us because our own consciousness is attracting it.

If we can feel a sense of gratitude for a spiritual message or for the avenue through which that message has been brought to us, and if out of the fullness of our hearts, that gratitude impels us to give our mite or our last penny, we shall find that there is no greater blessing than the experience of tithing. When it is the outpouring of sincere gratitude for the revelation of God as our individual experience, tithing is an expression of gratitude, and gratitude is one of the facets of love.

But there is an even stronger law than that which goes with tithing. Humanly, we believe that our present income is the extent of our supply, and humanly, we do not know how to increase it. When we begin tithing, however, we know that our tithe is not coming from *our* income, but from God. It is God's support of the activity of truth in human affairs, expressed in human ways.

Let us agree, then, to think of ourselves as transfer agents for good and contribute some specific sum of money every day or week to a spiritual purpose, not out of our income or the kindness of our hearts, but merely as instruments of God maintaining Its own infinite activity. When we do this, we soon find that not one penny of that tithe is coming from our own pocket and, furthermore, we shall find that eventually our income will increase, not merely sufficiently to be equal to the amount given but to go far beyond that.

Ultimately, we shall realize that and any every obligation— family or otherwise—is not our personal responsibility, but that of the Christ, and is, therefore, not to be met out of our personal income. No demand will be a drain upon our resources *if* we catch the central point that the demand is not being made upon us, but *upon the Christ*; and we shall look upon ourselves as instruments—transfer agents—through whom our family, friends, or relatives are supported.

Through our consciousness of the activity of God, Good, the Christ supports the activity of our life, bringing to us those who to our sense are avenues or channels of support, but always this will be the activity of the Christ *appearing* as these avenues or instruments. We must make a conscious decision to be transfer agents claiming possession of nothing ourselves, but merely being the instruments through which it flows. As soon as we are presented with a need, we recognize that the demand is made by the Christ on the Christ of us and that we can fulfil it, not out of our personal income, but out of that which the Christ gives us.

In the Bible, we are told that the widow had only a morsel, yet out of this morsel she was able to feed the prophet Elijah. Had the supply come from the little she had, it would never have sufficed. But the demand was not made on her personal supply: The demand was made on the Christ of her being.

A multitude of people sat around waiting to be fed by Jesus, but his disciples told him that there were only a few loaves and fishes. Unless he had been able to see that the demand was not on him but was a demand on the Christ Itself, that it was the Christ making a demand on the Christ, Jesus never could have fed so many people from the visible supply—never.

Jesus healed the multitudes, but if any person should interpret that to mean that a human being has enough understanding to heal a disease, heaven help the patient! Jesus never claimed such understanding or power. 'I can of mine own self do nothing[1] . . . The Father that dwelleth in me, he doeth the works.'[2] Every call for healing is a call upon the Christ, and all a practitioner can ever do is to be an avenue as which the Christ is acting to dispel the illusion of sense. It makes no difference if multitudes reach out to any one person for heal-

[1] John 5 : 30.   [2] John 14 : 10.

ing, because it would not be a human being responding, but the Christ acting or appearing as the person. The Christ, appearing as individual consciousness, can meet the demands of a thousand just as easily as of one. The Christ is unlimited.

No human being has any quality of his own that will produce a healing and no human being has enough money to support churches, practitioners, or teachers, but, as the Christ, any one of us could support a spiritual activity. We have only to accept the responsibility consciously: 'Father, I accept the responsibility to meet my generous share of the activity of the Christ-movement through me.' But that does not mean that we have the personal responsibility of supporting it. Our responsibility is to make the conscious decision that we are part of such work and that just as the Christ is operating as a spiritual lecturer, teacher, or writer, so that Christ is operating through us for the benefit of this whole Christ-activity.

It makes no difference whether we decide to give one, five, ten, or twenty per cent of our income. The point is that we must consciously make the decision to be a part of the spiritual activity of the world and to fulfil our part in it. If we are called upon for a healing or if we are called upon to speak from a platform, let us be ready, because it is only the Christ making a demand on the Christ, and any one of us could fulfil that demand by consciously making the decision to be a part of the Christ-life. There is a reason why all this is important, and it is not that of becoming healthier or wealthier human beings: It is that we may come into the realization of our Christ destiny and stop being just good human beings.

'The earth is the Lord's, and the fulness thereof.'[3] How much of that is yours? All of it! All of it, because 'Son, thou art ever with me, and all that I have is thine'.[4] Do you understand what I am trying to make you see? This is not for the purpose of making you a richer human being, but to make you aware of the fact that the entire kingdom of God is yours: 'The earth is the Lord's, and the fulness thereof.' All that belongs to the Father belongs to you: 'Son . . . all that I have is thine.' You will never know the allness of the Father while you are counting it in terms of dollar bills. You will know it only when you completely release yourself from the belief that you have, or have not, so much and begin to make the acknowledgment that all the earth belongs to the Father, and that all that the Father has belongs to you.

CHAPTER IX

HARMONY THROUGH ONENESS
WITH GOD

FOR several thousand years mankind has been told about its relationship with God and how to bring God into individual experience. The subject is old: The presentation is always new, always appearing in new forms. Truth is a state of infinite Consciousness, and because of that very infinity, it has infinite ways of presenting itself to us.

In the days of Krishna, probably the earliest recorded history of truth was given to the world in the form of the word *I*. Later somewhere around A.D. 800, Shankara culled out of the Oriental Scriptures that same secret, and again presented it by means of the word *I*. He went even a little further than recorded teaching up to that time and said, 'I am That; I am That', and his listeners naturally thought that here was a man who was calling himself God. But he really was not doing that at all: It was simply God announcing Itself to individual consciousness.

The one whom the Western world recognizes as Master—Jesus of Nazareth—presented the same story and proclaimed, 'I am the light of the world'.[1] Because of that, people said he made himself equal with God and thought it not unseemly to do the works of God, so they cried, 'Crucify him, crucify him'.[2] But all he really was saying was, 'I, the infinite Law of being, the infinite creative Principle of the universe—I am your very own consciousness. I am the very life of you. I am the very mind of you'.

He was not calling himself that; he was not calling a human being that. He was very careful to say, 'I can of mine own self do nothing[3] . . . My doctrine is not mine, but his that sent me'.[4]

[1] John 8:12.   [2] John 19:6.   [3] John 5:30.   [4] John 7:16.

He made a great distinction between the man who was appearing as the messenger and the I that was presenting Itself as the message. But the human mind was just as unwilling and unable to accept it then as it had been to accept it in its previous appearances on earth, and as it is to accept it today.

The revelation that the I is God, that God is the Soul of the individual, has appeared many, many times in the history of the world. Each time It has met with misunderstanding and sometimes with crucifixion. But It will continue to present Itself over and over again until we individually accept It and cease glorifying the human selfhood or think that it of itself is something great. It will present the same message in different forms until we so readily recognize It that we permit that little 'I' or ego to be crucified, 'to die daily', until it is completely out of the way.

If we wish to become one with this I and to bring It forth into our individual experience, we should know where to go to find it. We do not have to go to holy mountains, nor yet to that holy temple in Jerusalem. The kingdom of God is within our own being, and if we are to find it there, we must learn to see with inner eyes. Human eyes see only that which is plainly apparent. It is like looking at a musician playing, and believing that he draws music out of the instrument; but if we look with our understanding, we know that the music is drawn from the musical consciousness that is within his own being. The instrument is only an instrument, but the source of the inspiration, the source of the gift, is within the Soul of the individual, and that is God. One person brings It forth as music, another as architecture, and yet another as painting, but that gift is not outside in any mysterious God: It is always within the depths of our own being and is brought forth when we are able to put our worldly responsibilities in their proper place, to go within, and from that withinness to bring forth our particular gift.

Within each one of us there is a gift. According to Paul, there is only one Spirit that animates us all, but that Spirit brings Itself forth in different ways. One is given the gift of healing, another that of the law, and another that of preaching.

Each one, if he searches deeply enough within his own consciousness, will find some mode of expression uniquely his own. He may go outside to teachers for guidance and inspiration, but he cannot go outside to teachers to find the talent and ability that are already within him.

That same law holds true in spiritual living. We may go to a teacher or to a book for guidance and help along the way, but we cannot go to a teacher or to a book for God. For That, we have to go to our own Soul, to the innermost depths of our own being. No man, woman, or book can reveal God to us. All any one of them can do is to show us the path along which we may travel until we get back into the kingdom of our own being, the kingdom of our own Soul, and there find God.

It is like the disciple who went to his master and asked, 'Please, Master, show me God. Let me know God. Let me stand in God's presence.'

Over and over he made this appeal to his master, but the wise master did nothing about it except smile and say, 'Yes, in time, in time, in time'.

Then one day the master felt that the time had come, so he said to his disciple, 'I am going to take you to our secret and sacred temple. There are three rooms in this temple, but I can take you into the first one only. After that you will have to proceed by yourself. If you find the way, ultimately you will find God. If not, it will have to be another time.'

The disciple found himself alone in a room that was empty except for a golden statue of the Jehovah God, but after he became accustomed to the *feel* of this room, he sensed that something was wrong. 'No, this is not it. There is too heavy an atmosphere here. I shall have to go further.'

So he found his way into the next room, and after entering this second room, he began to breathe more freely. But as before, when he familiarized himself with the surroundings, he saw that he was once more in an empty room except for a crystal statue of the Jehovah God. He felt the lightness of that crystal; he felt the lightness of the atmosphere of the room, and said to himself, 'This is more like it'. But after a while he realized that this, too, was not It.

With that, he began to search for the entrance to the third room, and when he discovered it, he found himself in an empty room, a completely empty room. There was nobody there but himself.

That illustrates the search for God. We become one with God when we come into the realization that 'I and my Father are one',[5] but we have to turn within our own being to find that oneness. There is no other place to find happiness, peace, contentment, or security, except within our own being. Certainly, it cannot be found in wealth. There have been untold numbers of wealthy people who have not found happiness. In fact, no one of wealth has ever claimed that the wealth itself brought happiness. If there were not other conditions present, the wealth in itself was nothing.

Happiness is only to be found within. True, some people have found a degree of happiness in marriage, but only a degree. Until one finds within himself his own oneness with God, this sense of completeness because of the Father within, ultimately, there comes that same realization of incompleteness. Paul called this Father within the Christ. He said, 'I live, yet not I; but Christ liveth in me'.[6] Because he could tabernacle with that Christ, because he could commune with It and live with It, he had the secret of life.

John tells us of the temple not made with hands, the invisible universe. And where is that invisible universe? Where, except within our own being? And is it really invisible? No, it is visible and tangible—but only to the inner senses. This is the secret of life, and with the attainment of a realization and understanding of it, every scriptural promise and its fulfilment are ours. 'Lo, I am with you alway, even unto the end of the world.'[7] That is the invisible I, the invisible Presence—not present in the golden statue or in the crystal statue—only visible as emptiness to the outer senses, but completely satisfying and filling within. 'I am come that they might have life, and that they might have it more abundantly[8] . . . These things have I spoken unto you, that my joy might remain in you, and

[5] John 10:30.   [6] Galatians 2:20.   [7] Matthew 28:20.
[8] John 10:10.

F

that your joy might be full'[9]—full, filled full, fulfilled.

That I is God; that I is the Christ, the Son of God; and our conscious awareness of that truth is our communion between that which is our outer self and our inner spiritual Self. Some day, this outer self will disappear, and all that is left then will be the inner reality.

Spiritual living itself is the life lived by Grace—'not by might, nor by power'.[10] It is not a life of trials, tribulations, and hard labour. On the contrary, it is a life in which we find all things appearing to us in the order of our need of them, sometimes even before we ourselves are aware of the need. That is living by Grace, and that living by Grace is attained only when things and thoughts have been overcome. We have not overcome the world while we continue trying to improve or increase our material sense of the world. Having more money or having a heart or liver that functions as *materia medica* thinks it should is not the attainment of spiritual life or immortality. True, it is enjoying a better human experience, but at best it is a temporary one.

Spiritual life is that state of being in which we live by Grace, in which we know that an infinite invisible Presence, while not tangible to sense, does go out and if necessary provides even such unimportant things as a parking space for us or just the right hat or dress. We do not use It for that purpose, but It functions that way in our experience.

Jesus did not hesitate to call on It to produce transportation in the form of a donkey; he did not hesitate to call on It to bring forth gold out of the fish's mouth or to multiply the loaves and fishes. That he was not using this as a vaudeville trick or as a means of dispensing charity is evidenced in his response to those who came to him continuously for those loaves and fishes when he rebuked them as much as to say, 'You have come for more of the loaves and fishes, but why do you not try to understand the miracle behind it? Then you would not need these repeated handouts of loaves and fishes. I showed you the loaves and fishes and fed you with them so that you could see the principle involved. If you learn that

9 John 15:11.   10 Zechariah 4:6.

principle, you will have the invisible means of life.'

Jesus healed the multitudes, but he must have become very weary of it in the end because he said, ' "If I go not away, the Comforter will not come unto you."[11] Oh, I can do it! "My Father worketh hitherto, and I work."[12] I can do it, but if I go on healing all these ills of yours, what is going to happen to you? What is going to happen to you if you keep looking to a man called Jesus for your healing? What I am trying to say to you is, "The kingdom of God is within you." '[13]

Jesus called God your Father and my Father. He claimed no special right to God as Father. Very honestly and very openly, he referred to your Father and my Father and said, 'Greater works than these shall ye do; because I go unto my Father.'[14] Today, we in this age are listening to that selfsame message, the message of the Infinite Invisible. That which to the outer senses is intangible, but to spiritual consciousness is very real.

The secret of this inner life by Grace is that there are no yesterdays, there are no tomorrows—there is only the ever-present now. There is no penalty to pay for past mistakes, and neither are we piling up rewards for the future. We are living the fullness and completeness of life in this very minute. Now, in this minute, we are living. We cannot live yesterday and we cannot live tomorrow. The only thing that we can do is to live here and now this minute. And of course when tomorrow comes, it will be now also. It has to be now. It is all a continuous now—now—now. This minute is now. Next minute will be now. It is all now, and if we are living in the fullness of our understanding at this moment, we are doing all that can be expected of us. All that we are ever required to do is to forget the past, cease planning or worrying about the future, live to the highest sense of our spiritual capacity now, and leave the rest to God.

What we are living this minute will manifest itself in the next minute, the next year, the next era, or the next incarnation—if we consider the form of the continuity of life as incarnation or reincarnation. In some teachings, this is known as karma which is almost as true a teaching as there is in all

[11] John 16:7.   [12] John 5:17.   [13] Luke 17:21.   [14] John 14:12.

the world, and one which permeates all religious philosophies although under different names. In the Christian religion, this teaching is known as the law of *as ye sow, so shall ye reap*.

Regardless of what we may think about karma or about reincarnation, the truth is that life is eternal. The truth is that just as we are living now, so will we be living eternally— and we will be living life in whatever consciousness we ourselves unfold. Now, this minute, is the only life we have; right now, in this very minute, we have no past and no penalty to pay for a past:

Now I *am living in the fullness of God; now I am living in the fullness of love; now I am entertaining no animosity, no hate, no jealousy, no envy. There is at this very minute only love*—love for one another, love for the truth, love of God, love of the Christ.

All we have to do is continue in the consciousness of this minute, keep the love that is in our hearts this very minute— this love of God and desire for the understanding of the Christ that we know and feel at this very moment. With that love filling our being, there is no possibility of any other quality entering consciousness. We, and we alone, are responsible if we permit other thoughts to enter our consciousness. No one is responsible but our very own selves—yourself or myself. Is there any power in the world decreeing that we should hate or fear someone? Is there any power outside of us that can make us lustful, greedy, jealous, or envious?

A human being left to himself will never seek out God. Never! That is why there are always so few on this Path. There are only a few opening their consciousness to God. There always have been only a few and that was the reason why Jesus longingly cried, 'Oh, Jerusalem, Jerusalem,' as much as to say, 'I would love to do so much for you. I feel you are my little chicks. But why won't you open up your hearts and listen to me?'

Living by Grace means living by Love. There is no divine Love up in the sky; there is no divine Love going to come down and operate in us or through us or for us. The divine Love which supplies our every need is the love we express, the impersonal love which we express even to our enemy and to those who persecute us. As we pray for our enemy, we can watch how that divine Love very quickly meets our needs.

The story has been told about a woman who had a room to rent and who finally went to a practitioner for help, telling the practitioner that if only she had this extra ten dollars a week, all her needs would be supplied. Yet nobody came to rent the room during the entire week after her advertisement had appeared in the newspaper. The practitioner told her that she had approached the problem in the wrong way. 'You have been too much concerned about what you would *get*, what you need. Have you ever thought what that room could do for somebody living alone out in the world, someone who would benefit by the beauty or the harmonious furnishings of that room, by the spiritual atmosphere of your home, by the cleanliness, and by the high moral quality in your consciousness? Have you ever thought what would happen to a person who could move into that consciousness, who could have the divine protection of your spiritual consciousness? Go home and think about what your room could do for someone out in the world, and then see what happens.'

It was not long before a man came to look at the room, and noticed her metaphysical books on the table. After he questioned her about them, he said, 'That's a strange thing! I am also interested in such teachings, and I have been carrying your ad around with me for a whole week, but only today did the urge come to me to answer it.' The truth is that probably he had a higher sense of love than she had and was hoping or expecting to carry love to someone who was ready to express love, but not to someone who was just seeking ten dollars a week.

This love which you and I are to express cannot be expressed only to one another, for even the scribes and the Pharisees showered love on their families and friends. No, the love that we are called upon to express must be given to our enemies, to those who despitefully use us as well as to those who come within the range of our friendship and our home. The essence of love is oneness with God, and oneness with God makes inevitable the conscious expression of the qualities of God. There is nothing mysterious or occult about this. It is something we can do right where we are—in a bus, an automobile, or on an airplane. As long as we are looking out on this world with love and forgiveness and with joy that all who open their consciousness to the presence of God will in some manner bring It forth, that is all that is necessary.

Within us, there are greater capacities for joy than any of us have ever known in the external world. I myself have always been a voracious reader, but today I can find just as great a joy welling up within me as I can find outside in any book. Though I still enjoy good books, I find that if I am in a place where there are no books, all that could be found in books can be found in my individual consciousness. And so you would find it, too.

Peace, joy, power; 'My peace I give unto you: not as the world giveth, give I unto you.'[15] Money, home, automobiles, theatres, dances, and good food—that is the kind of peace that we get from the world. But My peace, the peace that I give which the world cannot give, is the peace we are seeking. That is the grace of God, and it is not outside of us to be achieved or acquired. It is already within us in the fullness, and always will be.

The Christ-peace, the presence of God, is with us, within our own being. But the world makes it very difficult for us to find that peace, and for that reason we must find it within our own being. We cannot find it in apartment houses or ocean-front homes. We have to find it within ourselves. And so it is with security. We cannot find security in our bank account. And just as we have to find peace and security within ourselves, so also do we have to find love, and the love we find is the love that we express.

Love is only one facet of God, just as truth is another. Here and now we are expressing truth, and the truth which we are accepting into our consciousness this moment will be with us

[15] John 14:27.

until the end of the world. All we have to do is consciously remember that, and then every word of truth will be a continuing prayer in our consciousness. It is up to us. We are the
master of our own experience, and we become that master
through this sense of *nowness*. To realize that the Christ of
God, the Son of God, is the very consciousness of our being
until the end of the world, and then to look out at all our
neighbours and realize that right there, too, is this same truth,
this same eternal life, this same love is fulfilling the two great
Commandments:

And thou shalt love the Lord thy God with all thy heart,
and with all thy soul, and with all thy mind, and with all thy
strength: this is the first commandment.
And the second is like, namely this, Thou shalt love thy
neighbour as thyself.

Mark 12:30, 31.

We can make this a continuing experience only in this
moment of Grace. The wholeness of the Godhead is flowing in
us and through us, and It is appearing here visibly as us. Let
us learn to look *through* what we see as a human face, and see
in everyone who presents himself to us the face of God—God
shining through, the grace of God appearing as every
individual.

In such a realization, *now* are we under divine Grace. All
of the time that existed before this minute is wiped out. So far
as we are concerned, there are no benefits from the past because in this *now* we need nothing from the past. We have the
fullness of the Godhead bodily in us at this very moment—the
fullness of God manifesting in, through, and as us this very
minute. Can we want more than that?

The Spirit of God, the presence of God in us, has lifted our
consciousness to something higher and better than even good
or happy humanhood, and we, here and now, dedicate ourselves to truth. Our body is the temple of the living God, and
we have dedicated it to the divine Life and divine Love which
is Its presence and power made manifest. There is no drawing

back. There is no withdrawing our body and taking it out of the presence of God, or taking God out of it. We cannot turn back a single moment. We have to realize from now on that we have been given the peace that passes understanding because of our own dedication to God, because we have brought our body as a temple to be dedicated to truth, life, immortality, spirituality.

What more can we do? Nothing. Nothing more is expected of us. When we reach out only one per cent to the Christ. It reaches out ninety-nine per cent to us.

At this moment we can drop our human concerns; we can drop our fear of whatever bodily, mental, or financial conditions seem to beset us. We have opened our door to God, to a receptivity to the divine Presence that goes before us to make the crooked places straight. That is all it takes—one little moment of dedication, one little moment of opening consciousness to this truth, and then realizing that what happens in this *now* is a continuing experience. It never stops, and it never will.

CHAPTER X

THE PRAYER OF UNDERSTANDING

ALL the good of an enduring and permanent nature that we ever attain is attained through the revelation of the Soul within. Only the Soul which is illumined finds peace, harmony, and wholeness in this human experience. Developed Souls are happy, successful, and prosperous people, because they have an awareness of spiritual values. Those of whom we say, 'Oh, poor soul!' are usually not only poor in Soul, but also poor in health, poor in spirit, and poor in purse.

From the time of the Old Testament to the present day, there have been many varying concepts of prayer. There have been prayers for the welfare of others as well as prayers for their destruction. It seems strange that anyone should pray to God to destroy something or someone, especially when it is difficult and oftentimes impossible to judge who is wrong and who is right. Such prayer, therefore, is really paganistic, but nevertheless it has been a widely known and practised form of prayer in the world.

As a matter of fact, it is not too long ago that we, as a nation, were guilty of praying for the destruction of one nation and then later joining it as an ally and, thereupon, praying for the success of its armies and then soon after praying for its destruction again. God must have laughed at that—if God knew and could laugh. If that seemed foolish to a human being with any degree of intelligence, how must it have seemed to God?

Before the Second World War, many people were aware that war was on the way, so they had been praying for many weeks that God would intervene and that war would not break out. But evidently God went about His spiritual business and paid no attention to those earthly supplications because the war came along practically on scheduled time. Throughout the war, there were days of prayer on which the people of our nation, and those of other nations as well, came together to pray for peace. Again God went on His way, and the war continued until the day came when the so-called enemy on the European front had exhausted its supply of ammunition and food. Then, and only then, did the war end.

When this happened, we were called upon to thank God because the war had ended. Many people must have been guilty of thinking that even if God had brought the war to a close, He had done a bad job of it. A bad job! Millions of people had been killed, maimed, and made destitute. How strange to thank God for ending the war in Germany when we all know that even while these people were in church thanking God for doing this, the same war was being bitterly fought in the Orient, and there, God was not doing a thing about it. Apparently He brought peace over here on this street, but to the war on the other street He paid no attention! And then one day He evidently decided to end that, too—just after the United States dropped two atomic bombs!

I am using this illustration primarily for the purpose of bringing to light the true nature and purpose of prayer. If, in this way, I can lead somebody to think about the kind of praying he is doing, my purpose will have been achieved. If we are praying for the end of some disastrous condition about which God knows nothing, it is time for all of us to stop and think seriously about this subject of prayer.

Volcanoes erupt; tornadoes lay waste the country; tidal waves wreak their havoc—and God goes on. Is there a connection between God and the terrifying and terrible events on earth? And if not, does that mean then that there is a condition apart from God? No, that could not be, since God is omniscient and omnipresent and God is good. It cannot be that *in reality* such experiences are going on; it cannot be that in God's kingdom men and women are dying or that men and women have died, or will die. Otherwise, God is failing, and that, in His main work which is eternality and immortality.

Prayer must have some purpose other than thanking God for

ending a war or thanking Him for our victory at another nation's expense. All wars have not always ended with those who were morally right being victorious. And yet the end of every war has always brought forth deep gratitude to God for bringing it to a close.

What, then, is true prayer? What should it be? How much of true prayer are we practising? How far are we failing in the right sense of prayer in this twentieth century even with all the enlightenment we have received in so many other areas? Prayer can never be successful until, and unless, we know what we are praying to, or praying for.

And that brings us to the subject of God. All prayers are uttered to God; all petitions are offered to God; all affirmations and denials are aimed at God. But what is God? Where is God? What is the function of God? Until we rightly understand the answers to those questions, we can never pray aright. We have been told that if we pray and do not receive an answer, it is because we have prayed amiss. Yet how many of us have been praying according to accepted metaphysical practice for years and years and years without getting an answer, and still we keep on praying in the same old way? It is time we woke up, is it not? It is about time we acknowledged that we have been praying amiss, that we do not know how to pray or for what to pray or to whom to pray or in what manner we must pray.

'By their fruits ye shall know them.'[1] If we are praying correctly, we are showing forth the fruitage of prayer in the degree of harmony, health, wholeness, prosperity, and success we express. I do not mean by that that just because a person has a healthy physical body or an abundance of this world's goods it is a proof that he is praying aright. There are many people who know nothing about prayer and yet who are physically healthy and materially wealthy. No, I mean that if we are praying aright, we are reaping the fruitage of the Spirit. And the fruits of the Spirit are love, well-being, peace, joy, and dominion—all spiritual qualities, not material things, but

[1] Matthew 7:20.

spiritual qualities which appear to us externally as a satisfactory physical universe.

The first question, then, that has to be answered within our consciousness is: What is God? Until that is solved, we will never know what prayer is. But I cannot define God—I doubt whether anyone can. I know many names for God, but these anyone can find for himself in the Bible and in metaphysical literature: God is love; God is mind; God is Soul; God is Spirit; God is life eternal. But these words do not tell us what God is. They only give us more names for the same word; they take one word and put in its place another, but they do not reveal what God really is.

No one will ever be able to tell us that, for that is something which is found within our own being. This is the reason that I believe that the purpose of prayer is the unfoldment of our Soul-faculties. As we go within our own consciousness with the question, 'What is God?' or ask, 'Father, reveal Thyself!' or, 'Speak, Father; Thy servant heareth,' we are really praying because we are turning within and asking God to reveal Itself to us, asking that our own Soul be revealed, be brought forth and enlarged.

True, God or Soul is infinite and, in the strictest sense of the word, cannot really be enlarged or developed. The apparent development lies in our unfolding awareness of that which already is infinite and omnipresent. Poetic licence enables us to use the expression 'the development or enlargement of the Soul' without really meaning that God changes or can be changed. We actually mean developing our *sense* of Soul, developing our conscious awareness of the nature and character of Soul or God. It is our sense that is enlarged, not God. God is already infinite. God is already omnipresent. But the omnipresence of God is of no avail except to those who come into conscious awareness of that Presence.

All the principles governing the operation of television and of the jet plane have always existed in consciousness and have been available, but they were of no use until someone caught the first glimpse and awareness of these principles and from there developed them and ultimately brought them forth in all their fullness. So it is with God. God is infinite; God is omni-present; God is omniscient; God is all-wise. But God becomes our protection and enlightenment only in proportion to our awareness of Him. Therefore, the first step in our spiritual experience must be to learn the nature of God, and in learning the nature of God, we are really praying. But an even higher form of prayer is attained when the human senses are entirely stilled, and the voice of God speaks to us, 'Be still, and know that I am God.'[2]

Many people think that when they are declaring that they are God, they are praying a very high prayer. Such prayer is atheism. It is trying to make a human being God and is an attempt to develop one's self, not through religion, but through psychology, making the human mind a power, making the human mind God. Those may be steps on the way, but it is only when our thinking, reasoning, human mind is entirely still and we hear a voice saying, 'Know ye not that I am God?' that we have reached a high form of prayer. Jesus uttered such a prayer when he said to Philip, 'Have I been so long time with you, and yet hast thou not known me, Philip? he that hath seen me hath seen the Father?'[3] Jesus, the man, had already disappeared out of his own consciousness, and all that was left there was God. Then he could say that to see him was to see the Father.

As long as we are indulging our hates, enmities, fears, and doubts, however, it is a little bit foolish to go around saying, 'I am God'; but it is a beautiful thing to develop an attitude of listening, an attitude of introspection and inner peace so that God can declare Itself. And God ultimately does just that.

In the metaphysical world, prayer and treatment have often been considered synonymous. There is a distinction, however, and while I am not trying to change the meaning standard usage has given these, nor finding fault with or criticizing any approach to metaphysics, to me the words *treatment* and *prayer* do not mean the same thing. To me, *treatment* is my declaration of truth, a way of reminding myself of the un-reality of error, and it includes my understanding of the nature

[2] Psalm 46:10.   [3] John 14:9.

of God and man. It may also be a recognition of the nature of spiritual law and a realization of the nothingness of that which appears as error in any form. To me, any thought that I entertain about the nature of God or man or power or error represents treatment.

Prayer, however, to me is the word of God. And the word of God is never uttered by 'man, whose breath is in his nostrils'.[4] The word of God is uttered only by God—the universal divine infinite Wisdom and Love—to the individual expression of God's being, you and me. As individuals, we are like the Prodigal Son who went away from home and set up a separate identity. So for the time being, we call ourselves Joel, John, Elizabeth, or Martha.

As long as I have a sense of a Joel separate and apart from God, I must turn within to that depth of me, that infinite unseen part of me which is God, and as I turn within, I hear It say to me, 'Son, all that I have is yours. We are one. I am in you, and you are in Me. We are not two: We are one. That which you are thinking of as your outer self is only the tiny little visible part of the infinite invisible Me. Do not set up that little thing out there called Joel and let him worry about his own life, his own supply, and his own home. I will take care of all that. Leave that with Me. Take no thought for your life, what ye shall eat. That is My responsibility—the responsibility of the infinite Unseen which is the creative Principle of all men.'

When I hear such a message of divine assurance within my own being, I know that the word of God is being spoken to me. And then the miracles begin! When that happened to Moses, manna came from the skies and water from the rocks. When the still small voice spoke to Elijah and Elisha, the ravens fed them and the dead boy was raised. All manner of miracles took place. Because Elijah and Elisha were so different? Oh, no, they had made their contact with God so that the voice of God was able to come through—that still small voice and that great infinite Power. That was the only difference.

What happened when the Father within came through

[4] Isaiah 2:22.

Jesus? It healed multitudes; It walked on the water; It disappeared through crowds and through walls; It preached the Sermon on the Mount. Finally It said, 'I have overcome the world.'[5] Those are the glorious things that can be done, not by you or by me, but by God—by God when we have prayed sufficiently, when we have heard the still small voice often enough, and when we have made of our human selves something of a vacuum so that that Thing can come through.

This is not a new message; this is the oldest message that has ever been on earth. There has never been a person of spiritual enlightenment who did not know this secret. It is found throughout the world—in the Catholic saints, in the Protestant saints, in the religious characters of the Hebrews, and in the great Hindu teachers. It is found in its full flower in the teaching of Jesus: 'I can of mine own self do nothing[6] . . . My doctrine is not mine, but his that sent me.'[7] It is heard when Paul speaks: 'I can do all things through Christ which strengtheneth me.'[8] Never has one of these people claimed anything of himself or for himself. Never has one of them said: 'My understanding is so great that I can move mountains'; but every one has indicated that in the degree that he could become a state of receptivity to the divine Power, It has performed miracles.

The true sense of humility is not hiding one's face and saying, 'I am nothing'. The true sense of humility recognizes God as infinite and supreme and realizes that God is pouring through, and then gives all credit and all honour to It.

Thou shalt have no other gods before me.

Exodus 20:3.

Cease ye from man, whose breath is in his nostrils: for wherein is he to be accounted of?

Isaiah 2:22.

5 John 16:33.   6 John 5:30.
7 John 7:16.   8 Philippians 4:13.

Put not your trust in princes, nor in the son of man, in whom there is no help.

Psalm 146:3.

All these quotations mean that God is not afar off. God is within you and within me, not actually existing inside physically, but within the realm or range of our consciousness. Ultimately, we discover that God is our very own consciousness, and as we learn not to use our thinking, reasoning mind, but to use that mind that was in Christ Jesus and allow It to be in us, then we feel the divine Impulse, we feel the divine Energy flowing through us and the divine Will being made manifest in our affairs.

We are servants of God, servants in the sense that we permit God to use our mind and body and Soul and Spirit and life for Its glory and Its manifestation, but not to set us up on high, nor to bring us a million dollars so the world can say, 'Hasn't he a lot of understanding?' No, all the good that comes to us is for the showing forth of the presence and power of God. And it is done through silence. Jesus washed the feet of the disciples in order to show them that he was a servant of God, not a master, but a servant, and when we learn to silence our personal will and desires, when we learn such a sense of humility that we are here in this experience as God's servants to show forth the glories of God and that we will never be satisfied to show forth inharmony or discord, then It happens.

Then why was it that Jesus fed the multitudes only a few times? Why did he not keep on feeding them continuously? Why did he not set up free kitchens all over the Holy Land to operate seven days a week and thus save the Hebrews the hard work of tilling the soil and harvesting their crops, even the hard work of marketing food?

He could have saved them a great deal of work. If he had just multiplied those loaves every day of the week, what an easy life those people would have led! But he did not think that was the function of the Messiah—of God or of the Christ. To him, his function was to reveal God in individual consciousness so that others could go and do likewise. Jesus realized that they were unable to see the principle behind the miracle so finally he had to rebuke them: 'I fed you yesterday, and now you are back for me. Why didn't you see the miracle yesterday so that you could do it for yourself today? You weren't looking for the principle; you were just sitting around waiting to be fed.'

Is it any wonder that he became weary and walked away from them to the other side of the lake? It must have been hard for him to see that all they were interested in was loaves and fishes. It is hard today to heal people, day in and day out, to heal them of colds and grippe and flu, corns and bunions and cancers and tuberculosis, and then ten years later have them come back and ask for another healing. The purpose of healing work really and truly is not just to make people well. It is to show forth the principle that exists as individual consciousness.

All the great metaphysical healers of the past century, Mary Baker Eddy, Myrtle Fillmore, and others who did really remarkable healing work and who left a substantial literature on the healing principles, probably had no thought of setting up a different form of *materia medica* to which people could turn for healing. I think those people expected that in one or two generations the whole world would be in metaphysics, and they had a right to expect it. But instead of that, what have we developed? A group of practitioners and a group of patients! This is sad because two thousand years ago the Master refused to set up a system merely of healing. He was not interested in healing only sick bodies and minds. He even rebuked his disciples, when they had cases that they were not able to heal, in some such way as this: 'Why, you have been around with me two or three years, and you still have not seen the principle. How long does it take you to learn this?'

It is not a difficult principle. The only difficult part of it for us in the Occidental world is to learn to be quiet long enough to hear the still small voice. Once we make the contact, from then on it is as easy as watching the gentle rains fall in spring.

It is not easy to raise the whole world or to heal everybody or even to heal ourselves of everything. We are dealing with

G

a mesmeric force in the world—universal belief—and it is impressive and powerful to the unenlightened even in its nothingness. It baffles and fools us—sometimes even the wisest of us. So far as I have observed, even the most spiritually enlightened once in a while come under that spell.

But the point is not whether we are demonstrating this one hundred per cent because even if we are demonstrating only ninety per cent of it now, we are doing very well; it is at least an indication that we are on the way, even though we cannot be satisfied with that. A principle to be a principle must be absolute, and that means that when we can catch this principle in its fullness and entirety, we shall have one hundred per cent healings. However, in this world of ours, it is not too long ago that our airplanes were using little two-lung engines which now have been increased to the multiple engines of the planes of today. We have gone from twenty miles an hour in one generation to two thousand miles an hour, and the end is not yet in sight. We will go on to greater and greater speeds.

So it is in the spiritual world. As far as demonstration is concerned, we are still partly in the human experience. We are still overly indulgent in our eating habits and overly protective in our attitude toward our family and friends. As we study the New Testament, we learn that we cannot come into the fullness of this vision until we have overcome our love and attachment for our mother, father, sister, and brother. That sounds strange for a religion of love, but it is true. The kind of love that we have to come into is the love which God has for the spiritual universe, a love that is impersonal and universal The only way to determine how far we have come along the spiritual path is to see if we are as willing to help the stranger down the street as we are our own brother or sister, or as willing to forgive somebody on the other side of the ocean as we are to forgive our own wife, husband, or son.

In other words, the overcoming of the human sense of love must take place, and this human love must be replaced with a sense of divine Love. Divine Love is the healer. When John said, 'God is love',[9] he did not mean the counterfeit that we

[9] I John 4:8.

call love, the kind of love that makes parents spoil their children and permit them to grow up as selfish adults, and sometimes even pursue a life of crime. That is not the love we mean when we speak of God as Love, nor is God-love the love that we entertain towards some person for a selfish purpose or motive. Love is that sense of being which is able to include the whole world.

This does not mean that we have to open our homes and make parasites of those who have not awakened to their true identity. It does mean, however, that we must be able to look through their human frailties and see the Divine in them and hold no personal animosity. The whole demonstration lies in our ability to give up our personal sense of love, hate, fear, and enmity. As we are able to do that, we are rising in spiritual consciousness, and that means that we are praying correctly.

True prayer is the development of the Soul. True prayer is reached when our Soul rises to such great heights that it says, 'Father, forgive them; for they know not what they do[10] . . . Neither do I condemn thee: go, and sin no more.'[11] That is divine Love. That is spiritual consciousness, and that nobody can develop for us but ourselves. The greatest teacher, the most spiritual of all masters, can lift us up towards the place where we desire it; he can help us to attain it; but ultimately it has to come from within our own being. 'This kind goeth not out but by prayer and fasting.'[12] Are we willing to fast from personal sense, from personal desires, personal hates, personal fears, and personal enmities?

In true prayer, we do not ask God for anything. Prayer should never be a going to God for something of a material nature. We should never turn to God for anything except the unfolding of our own Soul within our own being. That is the true sense of prayer—that God reveal, unfold, and disclose Itself to us, to our individual awareness. We can become aware of God and we can be as infinite as God is—only, however, to the degree that we lose personal sense.

The promise is, 'Son, thou art ever with me, and all that I

<hr>

[10] Luke 23:34.   [11] John 8:11.   [12] Matthew 17:21.

have is thine."[13] But we must make ourselves fitting temples for that. And the way we do it is not by making affirmations about God's goodness and our spirituality. It is by turning within and letting God reveal Its own being and identity. We shall find that as God fills our consciousness, so God fills what appears to us as an outer world, because the outer world is only the form of our inner world. Our inner world is the substance; the outer world is the form that that substance takes. Therefore, when consciousness is filled with the Spirit of God, then the outer form or human picture—the pocketbook, the health, the wealth, the home, and personal relationships—begins to take on spiritual, harmonious form.

Let us not waste time in these days ahead in praying to God to stop a war or to stop a depression. Let us not waste any time asking God to look down upon us and be merciful. It will not work. It has been tried for thousands and thousands of years. In Hindu Scripture, Hebrew sacred writings, and on into Christian Scripture, for many thousands of years, the prayer has gone out, 'O God, be merciful to me, a sinner! O God, be merciful! O God, forgive.' Let us understand that there is no such God. If there were, It would have been made manifest in earthly affairs centuries before this.

God is a law of love, and we have to come into conscious oneness with that God or law of love in order to benefit by It. How many people in metaphysics have tried to give this law of God to their children and found that they could not do it? Or to their brothers or sisters or mothers or fathers or husbands or wives? It is an individual experience.

Parents can join a Baptist church, and their children will be Baptists; they can be Catholics, and their children will be Catholics; but they cannot become metaphysicians and make metaphysicians of their children. True, it happens sometimes, but it happens only because those children had it within their own being to catch something that made them follow along that path. And if they do not catch it, they throw it all away, even though in later years they often return. Certainly, because where else can anyone go except to God when he gets

[13] Luke 15:31.

into enough trouble? But this all proves that it is an individual matter. No one can become a metaphysician of any school by inheritance. If there are parents, Sunday School teachers, or practitioners who are able to impart enough of this wisdom to children so as to set up in them a desire for it, these children may hold to the truth when they become adults. But barring that, a person will have to wait until he himself is ready to turn to God.

For us to sit around praying for all the peoples of the world to be spared from war when in their hearts and souls some of these very people are plotting and planning another one will not work. Ninety-nine per cent of the prayers of the world are never answered because they are not prayers, and because they are uttered to a non-existent God, ignorantly worshipped. What the world needs is Abraham Lincoln's prayer—not that God be on our side, but that we be on God's side.

We are one with God as we ourselves are the outlet for that divine Love, that Love which passes understanding, that Love which is grace, gentleness, peace. God is infinite intelligence, and we are one with God in proportion as we open our consciousness to be led by that infinite intelligence—'not my will, but thine, be done'.[14]

If I have made it clear only in a tiny measure—a measure as large as a grain of dust—that our concept of God must be changed and that we individually have to begin the work of conscious at-one-ment, my whole life will have fulfilled itself. To catch a really higher concept of God than I have now, so that I can feel just a bit closer to this almighty Spirit which is the reality of my being, is the great purpose of life. I know It will use Itself through me for some good end, but I also know right well that I cannot go out on street corners and preach this. I feel very, very fortunate if the few who are drawn to me can catch one little glimpse of what I am trying to say, and if in them I can bring to life a little bit of the Spirit that will speak to them in these words, 'Change your idea of prayer; do a little higher praying and have a little higher concept of God than to believe that He began a war or that He is ever going

[14] Luke 22 : 42.

to end one or that He is ever going to forgive anyone his sins while he is still in his sins.'

Forgiveness is accomplished only by the forsaking of the sin. There is no other way. It is no more possible to be forgiven while indulging in the sin than it is to continue believing that 3 x 3 is 8 or that 4 x 4 is 19 and expect the principle of mathematics to take the gentle and forgiving attitude, 'Well, after all, you are a charitable soul, so we will give you the correct answer.' It is not done—not in mathematics, not in music, not in painting, art, sculpture, or writing. Those who turn to science and the arts must turn to them fully open to their principles. Those who turn to God must turn to God with a complete openness of consciousness to It.

Does that mean, if we are indulging some sin or sickness or hate, envy, or jealousy, and we cannot humanly stop it, that we are damned? No! It does not mean that at all. As a matter of fact, I think most practitioners would be willing to admit that it is much easier to work with a healthy sinner—one who at least knows that he is a sinner and that he is not deriving too much good from his sinning so he is perfectly willing to let go of it if it can be made possible for him to do so—than with a so-called good and pure human being. In that spirit of emptiness, it is very easy for a person to experience Grace, salvation, and healing. The person who is convinced that he is perfect just because he happens to be a pretty good human being has no real sense of humility. None at all! The real sense of humility is found in Jesus' statement: 'Why callest thou me good? there is none good but one, that is, God.'[15] In that sense, we can agree, 'Well, if that is the case, then I need a great deal more awareness of the Father in order to wipe out even some of my human goodness.'

This approach to God does not create in us a hopeless attitude because for the moment we are unable to give up our hate, envy, greed, or lust. These negative qualities will not be a deterrent to our spiritual progress if we have come to a place in consciousness where we realize that they are not as desirable as we once thought them to be and that we want to be rid of

[15] Matthew 19:17.

them. From that point on, salvation is certain. It may sometimes be slow because we have lessons to learn, but it is *certain*.

There must be an acknowledgment of our own lack of spiritual perception and a recognition of something above and beyond us; there must be an emptying out of the false ego; there must be the willingness to turn within. Then, as we feel and realize God within us, we are very close to the ultimate of prayer—hearing the still small voice and being consciously directed in all our ways.

Instead of constantly praying for humanity and praying to stop wars, let us forget about that for a while, turn within for a realization of the presence of God, and see That out picture Itself, not only in our experience, but in the experience of those around us. Then let the circle spread from there until ultimately it takes in the world. That will bring peace on earth —and only that.

CHAPTER XI

SPIRITUAL LIVING

SPIRITUAL living is not a way of life that will separate us from our present experience, nor will it take us out of our present activity except as we progress. True, it may lift us up into the practice of spiritual healing, or into teaching and lecturing on spiritual subjects, but it will not necessarily remove us from our present life experience. It will merely enhance the beauties and increase the safety and security of the life we are now living.

Jesus taught—and it is on his teaching that The Infinite Way is based—that we are not to leave this world, that we are to be in the world but not of it. We are to be in the world and enjoy liberty, freedom, happiness, contentment, peace, joy, and dominion. He did not say anything about going out into the wilderness and becoming an ascetic; he did not teach going apart from the world and living in the universe removed from the problems of every-day life. Rather, he increased the very loaves and fishes that the people were accustomd to eating. He brought forth gold from the fish's mouth, the same gold that was used as currency in those days.

So is it with the spiritual way of living. It is not meant that we should live in poverty, but rather that we should live in infinite abundance without any limitations except the limit of our own ability to *accept* that abundance. There is no sin in money or in wealth: The sin is in the love or hate of it. It is right for us to be abundantly supplied, but in the spiritual way of living, the concept of wealth must be changed from the material to the spiritual.

Suppose we assume that our income comes from our work. The spiritual way of life does not interfere with our income, whether from work, investments, or marriage; but it does prevent our believing that such a source is really the source of the supply. It may be the *avenue* of supply to us, but not the *source*. In the spiritual way of living our reliance is not on the money, the job, the investment, or the husband or wife. Our reliance is on the Source of the supply, which is God, the divine Consciousness of our being. In the spiritual life, we change our belief that money or investments constitute the source of our income. We change that belief to the understanding that God, the divine Consciousness of us, is our supply. Then the money that comes is the added thing, just what those loaves and fishes, and the gold out of the fish's mouth were to Jesus. We do not hoard our resources. We utilize them, save or invest them.

But whatever we do, we no longer fear the absence or lack of money; we no longer have concern about how much of it we have because we know that God is the source of it. If God is the source, that Source will always be there, and as long as the Source is there, the supply will be there. And since God has no beginning or end, does it make any difference whether we are in the prime of youth or approaching old age?

As long as we exist, we are the law of life and the law of supply in action; we are our own master; and we are the law unto our supply, the life and the intelligence of our supply. Therefore, our supply will be continuous.

As long as anyone thinks of dollars as his supply, he will not demonstrate the law of supply. A person must make the transition to where he understands, 'As long as I am alive, I, myself, am a law unto my supply, and because of that, the dollars must appear as a result of the law which I am.' Were we to permit our attention to deviate from that truth, were we to go out and think of people as our supply, sooner or later that supply would not be there, sooner or later something would show us that our faith had been in 'princes' and that 'princes' have failed us. We are not to put our faith 'in man, whose breath is in his nostrils';[1] we are not to put our faith in dollars or in investments. Faith must be in the law of God, which we are.

[1] Isaiah 2:22.

The same is true of health. It is right for us to be healthy, although neither material riches nor physical health will bring us immortality, because no matter how healthy our body is according to medical standards, we have no assurance of that health tomorrow or at sixty, seventy, or eighty years of age.

The goal of the spiritual way of life is not so much to improve our physical health as to establish health in the body through spiritual means and then to maintain it through spiritual means. But as long as we believe that our heart, liver, lungs, stomach, or any other part of our body has power or jurisdiction over our life, just that long are we in slavery or in bondage to the physical sense of existence, which means birth, age, decomposition, and eventually death.

This vicious circle from birth to death will go on in our individual experience as long as we carry the age-old belief that our life is in our liver, heart, lungs, and stomach, or that our body is a governing factor of our life. The spiritual sense of life reverses that and says:

The consciousness which I am forms this body, and that consciousness keeps on unfolding and unfolding unto eternity. If I desire to remain on this plane for one hundred, two hundred, or five hundred years, I can. It is possible to accomplish this because life is eternal.

Many people accept the idea that life is eternal, but not the idea that the body is eternal. In the spiritual sense of life, however, life and the body are one. Life is the substance, and the body is the form as which that substance appears. Suppose we had a great block of mahogany and out of that piece of wood we formed a desk. Mahogany would be the substance, and desk would be the form. And if the question arose as to how long that desk could last, we would know that it would last as long as the mahogany lasted, and that when the mahogany came to an end, the desk would come to an end. Desk is merely a name given to mahogany appearing as that particular form.

Each one of us must come to the realization that life is what we are. Life is what is looking out from back of our eyes—

Consciousness, Spirit, Soul. That is why it is said that the eyes are the windows of the Soul. What the world sees as us is the form in which that consciousness appears. If we can hold to that despite the mesmerism of world beliefs, then we can maintain ourselves here in this form as long as we can hold to that realization. Accepting the mesmerism of the world belief in a life limited to three score years and ten or the human belief of being lonesome because all our friends and relatives have gone on, and there is a new generation, keeps us from this realization.

Temptation lies on every side, so we have to be very alert when we adopt the spiritual way of life. It is not always a material circumstance or a physical illness that hypnotizes us, but often these invisible little 'foxes' like lonesomeness and fear. We exist as consciousness, infinite spiritual consciousness, and our body is the form which consciousness has fashioned in order to express through the individual its infinite form and Spirit.

The spiritual way of life is not one human mind telling another human mind how to be better; it is not being merely a good man or woman. In fact, becoming a good person will not of itself lift anyone into the spiritual life. In the spiritual way of living, we do not try to become merely better human beings. We turn to the Christ and let that Spirit erase all the disease, poverty, and sin. Only the state of consciousness that knows the nature of God can bring permanent peace, joy, harmony, and wholeness.

As long as we think of God as something separate and apart from our own being, we will not attain the spiritual life. God is divine consciousness and, because God is infinite, God is the consciousness of every individual.

'Closer is He than breathing, and nearer than hands and feet.'[2] How close is that? Right here, right where I am. Where God is, I am. 'I and my Father are one.'[3] This Consciousness which is infinity is my consciousness, and therefore wherever

[2] Alfred, Lord Tennyson, *The Higher Pantheism.*
[3] John 10:30.

*God is, I am. If I make my bed in hell, whom shall I fear? I
cannot get away from God because God is the very consciousness of me, and I cannot get away from my own consciousness.*

Yet, if that is true, why are any of us ever in a state of sin,
sickness, death, or limitation? Because we do not know this
truth; because we do not know and follow the little prescrip-
tion that Jesus gave us, 'Know the truth'. He never said the
truth alone would make us free. He said, 'Ye shall know the
truth, and the truth shall make you free.'[4] It is our continuous
knowing of the truth that makes us free.

Truth is right here in this very room. All the music, all the
languages, all the skills are right in this room, but until we
let the truth, or understanding, of any one of them into our
consciousness we cannot be musicians, linguists, sculptors, or
architects. So with God. Only in the degree that we accept and
really understand His word—feel and gain the conviction of
God as the reality of our being, feel this oneness, this contact
—only in that degree can we prove the law that says that no
harm can come to us, that no weapon that is formed against us
can harm us. That must sound absurd to people who are being
wounded and hurt because there are many weapons being
formed against them and they are being badly harmed. As a
matter of fact, it would appear that the weapons are winning
out.

But in the Bible we read: 'No weapon that is formed against
thee shall prosper.'[5] To whom is that addressed? Only to those
who accept and have the actual conviction of the presence of
God. All the others are of the 'thousand that shall fall at thy
side, and [the] ten thousand at thy right hand'.[6] But certainly
no weapon that is formed against those who know God can
prosper. There is no place where the presence of God does not
exist, from the bottom of the seas to the topmost sky, but it
is the conscious awareness of God that is the all-important
factor, and that is what makes for spiritual living.

From the moment that we achieve this conscious awareness
of the presence of God, something wonderful begins to happen.

[4] John 8:32.   [5] Isaiah 54:17.   [6] Psalm 91:7.

We can violate all the laws of *materia medica* when we have the conscious awareness of the presence of God because they are only beliefs, not laws, changing every few years. If a doctor were asked whether he practised medicine according to the medical books of many years ago, he would laugh, for today *materia medica* itself laughs at many of those things it believed a generation ago. We become free of world beliefs as we individually renounce them and begin to understand that they do not exist as law, but as beliefs. That is the secret of spiritual healing. We stand so completely in control of our own being and body that we understand that God acting as our infinite Intelligence is a law unto all our experiences and nothing can enter to defile it or to make a lie.

This means that we have come into the realization that nothing of this world has power; nothing in this world, whether in the form of thought or thing, has jurisdiction, government, or control over us. We are in the world, but not of it. We can enjoy the theatre, good music, and the companionship of friends; we can enjoy vacations, trips to the mountains or the seashore, and yet be so untouched by all of it that if the opportunity to do these things did not arise, we would feel no sense of loss.

Are you beginning to catch just a little glimpse of the fact that spiritual living has nothing to do with taking from us our normal or natural way of living? It will not make ascetics of us, except that we will be untouched by the world—in it, but not touched by it. We can have all the health and wealth in the world, and yet not dissipate it. We can enjoy all the good things in the world today, and yet not miss them if they are removed from us.

Spiritual living is a recognition of the presence of God as our individual life, not seeking the good things of life, but letting them be added; it is the realization that the thoughts and things of this world cannot enter our consciousness to defile. They have no presence or power over us and find no outlet through us. All that flows out from us is love, not our love, but God's intelligence, not our intelligence, but God's. All the good anyone expresses is God showing through, but the moment we think of any intelligence, any skill, any virtue, or any demonstration as being an evidence of our understanding, then our senses are warped, and we are heading for trouble. There is nothing good but God. There is no one loving but God. And this is spiritual living.

Let us not go up into the stratosphere and believe that our spiritual life in any way separates us from peace, contentment, and fulfilment, but let us live our lives as normally as possible and get all the joy we can out of human companionships. We do not break the ties of human relationship, but bring them to a higher level when we understand that God is the life of our husband, wife, child, or friend. In this way we form a bond much closer and more meaningful than any blood or affectional tie.

CHAPTER XII

SPIRITUAL FREEDOM

THE spiritual way of life leads to spiritual freedom, which is a quality or condition of being that comes as the result of the attainment of Truth Itself.

In the material sense of life, the world is in bondage—in bondage to hundreds of different thoughts and things. There is no denying this, although metaphysicians are very likely to claim that there is no bondage in God. That, of course, is true. There is no bondage in God, but it is also true that if you were living in God, you would not find it necessary to read a book on this subject. It is only because you and I have not yet reached the life which is God that we are interested in the way to achieve it.

The term way has a long and interesting history. Jesus said, 'I am the way.'[1] Lao-tze's teaching 600 years before the time of Jesus was called The Way. The way refers to that spiritual path that gives us freedom, but the very use of the word freedom implies a freedom from some form of bondage. In reality, there is no freedom in Spirit or Soul because there is nothing to be free of: There is only divine Being.

It is not easy for anyone to understand or even to explain the subject of spiritual freedom. In fact, it might be possible to grasp the Einstein theory more easily because this requires the developing of the human mind to the degree of grasping and understanding higher mathematics. No one, however, can ever develop his thinking human mind or intellect to the point where he will be able to understand Spirit and spiritual activity.

There is a Power greater than any of the powers with which we are familiar in the human sense of life, a Power that we can never see, never hear, taste, touch, or smell. It is a Power

[1] John 14:6.

that we can discern only with our spiritual senses, and if we cannot be lifted up to the point of spiritual discernment, we shall never know the meaning of spiritual freedom. We are, therefore, touching this subject from the standpoint of opening our consciousness to the recognition and the discernment of a Presence and a Power that we cannot see. Nevertheless, we can see the results of it in much the same way as we might be able to see the development of a seed in the ground, if we could see it through a microscope, but we never would see the life or activity *producing* what we see even through a microscope. In other words, we could watch the seed break open and the little formations come out; we could watch the roots take hold and the shoots come forth, but never could we see the life or the power, that which we know as *nature*. We never can see *nature* or the activity of *nature*: We can see only its results.

And so in this spiritual life, even when we have attained or are attaining spiritual freedom, we never actually see what is bringing it about. But as our consciousness of truth opens, as this seventh sense develops within us, then we shall be able to enjoy spiritual freedom and, in our higher moments of illumination, be able to see the whole of its operation. 'Yet in my flesh shall I see God.'[2] According to this scriptural promise, it is possible while yet being in what we call the human sense of life to behold God, but not to behold God with the eyes. We behold God through that seventh sense—spiritual consciousness or spiritual discernment.

Let us now consider the idea of bondage to a person, place, or thing. The mother who is continuously in fear of what will happen to her child and cannot let the child out of her sight is in this bondage. She is in bondage to mother-love; she is in bondage to fear of a power apart from God, to fear that there is a power that can prevent God's protection from being made manifest. That is one form of bondage.

Another form of bondage is fear of leaving familiar surroundings, keeping us tied to the place where we were born—to the city, state, or country. This form of bondage will not permit us

[2] John 19:26.

to be pioneers, to live where we want to live, or to build in some other place.

Bondage to a pay check often causes us to work under conditions that are not harmonious or that do not make for happiness. We work for people who do not understand us because we feel that we need the money. There is no denying our need for the money, but there certainly is a need to deny the necessity of our being in bondage to a particular place of employment. This bondage consists of our acceptance of the *belief* that we cannot break free and seek employment elsewhere, that we cannot seek fulfilment in some kind of work where we would be happier or freer. Remaining in a place where we of our own volition would never remain, or remaining in some activity where, if we could choose, we would not remain, is bondage.

Bondage to dollars comes from the belief that dollars are power, purchasing power. To human sense, that is true, but actually the power is in our own being. The dollars are a medium of exchange just as streetcar transfers are. True, the dollars have a greater value, but they are also forms of exchange, and we can have as many of them as we can open our consciousness to accept. We must attain freedom from the belief that power and supply are in the dollar, and transfer that power to our own consciousness in the realization that the supply is within our own consciousness, governing this world of dollars. Then automatically we break the bondage to dollars which really is a fear of a lack of them.

The Bible says, 'The love of money is the root of all evil.'[3] The love of money, the hate of it, or the fear of it is the bondage. That is the evil—not the money itself. There is nothing wrong with money. Money is a useful thing, just as useful as good clothing or speedy transportation, but the moment we give it power or dominion over us, we have lost our spiritual freedom.

There is bondage to superstition—not only the fear of walking under a ladder or of breaking a mirror, but other forms of superstition, such as theological or medical superstitions. One

[3] I Timothy 6:10.

H

of the great fears of many people is that they will live only three score years and ten. That is a pernicious form of bondage because, when that thought grips us, we begin soon after our fifties to wonder if we will ever reach seventy, and worry about how dreadful that will be.

There is the law of heredity which is not a law, but a fear or a belief. The ancient Hebrews believed that the sins of the fathers were visited on the children unto the third and fourth generations, yet two hundred years later they renounced that belief. But in this modern age we have not accepted their renunciation; rather have we accepted their old superstitious belief, and we are walking around with diseases and habits we think are due to heredity. Accepting certain forms of limitation for ourselves because of racial, religious, or national inheritances is a form of bondage.

Many people in this world are in bondage to their sins. These are the ones who seem to be the most miserable of all because their old religion and theology have impressed on them that they have sinned against some law, usually some foolish man-made law, and that they are going to be eternally damned, not only here on earth but even unto the future kingdom. That is a form of bondage too, a very, very acute form of it.

Millions of people are in bondage to the belief in infection, contagion, and climate, a bondage from which it is very hard to free themselves because they honestly believe that these things affect them. They do, on the human level of life, but the truth is that these theories are not of God. They are facts to be coped with only in the human sense of life. But the human sense of life is the bondage from which we must free ourselves. The whole human sense of life, even when it is good, is a form of bondage.

Together with these beliefs come all the beliefs incident to the human organism—the belief that there is life in the heart, or that when other vital organs are not functioning properly life is impaired. Of course at that point, someone may say that it is not our life that is impaired but our body. What I am saying is that our life is not impaired, nor is our body, except in proportion to our own bondage to the beliefs of materiality, the belief that the organs and functions of the body can contain within themselves the issues of life. That is a form of bondage to the body that has to be broken.

The antidote to all these forms of bondage is the First Commandment: 'Thou shalt have no other gods before me'[4]—no other power, no other presence, no other life, no other mind, no other intelligence, no other directing force, but God. Anything else is idolatry and is placing faith and power in an effect.

One of the most important things for all of us to understand is that we are not in the world. The belief that we are is a form of superstition and a form of bondage. *The world is within us!* It is a formation of the infinite Consciousness which we are. It is a form of divine Being which has been created by that universal Intelligence which really is our individual consciousness. We ourselves created the heavens and the earth—the consciousness which we are—and therefore they are subject unto us. Let us then be done with bondage to anything that exists in the realm of effect.

Our only bondage, if bondage it is, and it is a beautiful one, is to the Christ—the divine idea of government, the divine idea of infinite intelligence—and this is the only thing unto which we are subject. Divine Consciousness, universal Consciousness, that which we call God, which is individual consciousness, yours and mine, in the law of individual being. Through that, we are given dominion over all that is in the sea, the earth, the air, and the sky. When we either knowingly or unknowingly permit something in the realm of effect to be a law unto us, we have placed ourselves in bondage to it.

For the world at large, there is an excuse. The world at large has never been told that every person is a law unto his own being. The world has known a God only somewhere off in the skies or on a cross, and for centuries it has been taught that man is a worm of the dust, that he is a mortal, or that he is a human being, subject to all these different influences. Since it has accepted that teaching, not knowing any better, we cannot blame the people of the world when they come under the bondage of these material and theological beliefs. But for you

[4] Exodus 20:3.

and for me, there is no excuse. We know our true identity; we know that we are joint-heirs with Christ, that all that God has is ours; and we have been taught that this applies literally and unconditionally to you and to me today, not merely to the great Master Christ Jesus of some two thousand years ago. Therefore, for us there is no excuse when we knowingly bring ourselves under bondage to these man-made beliefs and so-called laws.

There are many other forms of bondage that we come under through ignorance because we have not progressed far enough in the study and practice of truth. We are really only at the first outer rim of the subject; we are far from being at the centre. There is probably much that we do not understand and because of that lack of understanding we remain in bondage. But there is so much that we do know and do not consciously practise that at this point it becomes necessary to ask ourselves, 'How many superstitions am I accepting? How many phases of bondage am I accepting? Even with the little understanding that I have, should I not be freer?'

Freedom begins when we recognize that God is divine consciousness, and that His consciousness is yours and mine. From that moment on, I and the Father are not only one, but consciously one. It has always been true that everybody is one with the Father, but not having the conscious awareness of it has made it impossible for the manifestation to come forth. In other words, our freedom comes not because of our relationship with God: It comes because of our *conscious awareness* of that relationship. The relationship which in reality exists between God and every individual in the universe is oneness, but that will not halt the building of jails, hospitals, and insane asylums because no one can benefit from his relationship with God except in proportion to his conscious awareness of it.

'Thou wilt keep him in perfect peace, whose mind is stayed on thee.'[5] That passage should be brought to our remembrance over and over again because in the conscious awareness of the presence of God and in the conscious awareness of our true identity lies our freedom. Nothing external to our conscious-

[5] Isaiah 26:3.

ness has power over us. In reality, there is nothing external to consciousness.

What we see as a person is not reality. We are seeing only the universal concept of the individualization of God. But even that concept which we see has no jurisdiction over us, no government, not even for good; nor has any *effect* in the external world any power or dominion over us. In other words, our consciousness itself is the power unto all formation, and through that knowledge it becomes the power over every concept of every formation.

For example, the lungs, heart, and stomach are not divine realities. God did not create them. They are universal concepts of some divine idea, some divine faculty or activity, but in the understanding that the infinite divine Consciousness which I am is the law unto Its spiritual creation, we are brought into dominion over even such concepts as lungs, heart, and stomach. That is the basis on which spiritual healing operates. It is the realization of God, divine Consciousness, as the substance, law, and cause of all spiritual creation. The knowledge of that truth gives us dominion over our concept of spiritual creation.

God is Spirit, and therefore, the universe is spiritual; but that universe of God cannot be seen except in our moments of spiritual illumination. Through our developed spiritual consciousness, we may then behold it; but in our everyday life, we never come into contact with either God or God's creation: We come in contact with the world or race concept of that creation, but our knowledge of the truth of God as infinite Being, the one Power, and of all creation as subject to that Power, gives us dominion over this world of concepts.

Therefore, when we take the first step toward spiritual freedom, we do it by consciously realizing that nothing appearing as the external world is a power over us, whether it is a heart, a brain, a germ, a bit of food, or even an atomic bomb. Our first sense of freedom must come when we consciously accept the truth that nothing out here has power over us except in proportion as we give it power. It, of itself, has no power, but we, by fearing it, give it power.

We might see a chair with a white sheet thrown over it and

assuming it to be a ghost, tremble all night and eventually die of heart failure, but this would not be because it had any power over us—only because we, in not perceiving it as it is and through believing that something external could have power, gave it the power to govern and control us. Someone might ask, 'Well, that's true of the chair with the sheet over it, but suppose it really were a ghost?' The same thing would apply. Even if there were such a thing in existence as a ghost, it could exist only as the effect of consciousness. Therefore, it cannot be a power over the consciousness that produced it. We ourselves impart power to these effects, and only in that degree do they have power over us.

There are almost innumerable forms of bondage which hold us in virtual slavery to fear. We are afraid of dictatorship in government and we are afraid of man-made laws of every name and nature, instead of realizing that we ourselves constitute all the law there is. The law abides within our own consciousness. When we know that, we can be free regardless of what form of government may appear. It really does not make any difference. There are men in slave countries who are free. All those who are able to accept their freedom within their own consciousness are free.

Bondage lies in our superstitions, in our belief and acceptance of a presence and a power apart from God. But when we can accept in our consciousness the idea that God created us free, that God gave us dominion, in that moment the world recognizes our freedom and makes way for us. We ourselves control the world's reaction to us, and do so by our own estimate of our own being.

Bondage is in one's own belief, and that is the only place where it is. If we are entertaining a sense of bondage to person, place, thing, circumstance, or condition, it is in our own consciousness, and that is where we have to meet it. It is up to us to develop the degree of freedom we want to enjoy. We have to learn that God is infinite intelligence, and that intelligence is our intelligence. We are all equal before God; we are equal before God *and* man.

The Christ is not a Christian; the Christ is not a Jew, the

Christ is the divine Spirit of individual being and is the Spirit of God in man. Everybody has It regardless of race or religion. But unless you and I consciously accept It, we will not express It, and, if we do not consciously accept It, those with whom we come in contact cannot feel It. Every time we go into a restaurant or a place of business, we feel the state of consciousness of the person who serves us. We recognize it for what it is.

When we can arrive at the place where we realize that nothing in the external world has power over us for good or for evil, we are able to bring our attention and thought back to that which is within our own being—reality. We can then turn within in meditation or communion and there find the Father.

How many times we have read in the New Testament about the Father within! How many times we have read what Paul said: 'I live; yet not I, but Christ liveth in me.'[6] But how seldom have we sat down with ourselves and felt that we must get acquainted with this Father within and find out what Paul meant. Most of us never find the Father within, the Christ. Those who do usually are on the metaphysical or spiritual path, but even there few ever really investigate and find out if what Jesus said is true. It is only through conscious effort that we contact the Christ or the Father within our own being, but until we do, we cannot gain spiritual freedom. Spiritual freedom does not come from statements of truth that we may know, nor through knowledge gained intellectually. Spiritual freedom itself is attained when we touch the Christ of our own being and actually feel the divine Presence within us.

We are dealing with reality, with that which is invisible to our outer senses and which therefore must be met within our own consciousness, and each one has to do that for himself. There is no easy road; there is no royal way. There are helps on this way, however, in the form of spiritual literature, teachings, and teachers, but the Christ is the way which leads us to the kingdom of God.

Jesus told his followers very frankly, 'If I go not away, the Comforter will not come unto you.'[7] It is a good thing to have

6 Galatians 2:20.   7 John 16:7.

practitioners and teachers, but it is not good to have them for too long. It is a great comfort to be able to lean on somebody on this spiritual path for help, guidance, and healing, but it does not make for individual growth to keep on leaning and leaning and leaning and never find our spiritual freedom.

In some religious teachings, there are those known as masters, just as in the ancient days Jesus was called Master. A master is one who has achieved some measure of spiritual freedom, which means some measure of nonattachment to the things and thoughts of the world. People often get the idea, however, that the function of a master is to take over another's mind and life and to govern and manage them for that person, but a master is one to whom a person can go and through whose help and co-operation he can be lifted up into a state of spiritual consciousness and discernment where he himself realizes the Master in his own consciousness. The Master is not a man: The Master is a state of unfolded and developed consciousness.

Jesus possessed this Master-consciousness probably to the greatest degree ever known, but people today seldom think of Jesus' consciousness. Instead, they go about using the name Jesus Christ and repeating it as if the name of itself had a virtue. And they claim that the reason the name has virtue is because it was the name of the Master of Galilee and therefore was imbued with his great spirit.

That the name of this Master of Galilee was Jesus Christ is open to question. Jesus and Christ are both Greek words, and there probably never was any Hebrew in Galilee with a Greek name. Christ is not a name. It is a title. Christ is the Saviour, the divine Consciousness; and Jesus was not Jesus Christ, but Jesus the Christ. The man Jesus was a Hebrew; in Aramaic named Joshua, not Jesus. If the name Jesus Christ were the name of a man who had attained mastership, certainly the *name* did not attain mastership. It was the consciousness that attained mastership, and nothing but that consciousness should be the Master unto us.

The Master is the divine state of consciousness, and one which you and I may attain, but only in the degree to which we lose our hate, fear, and love of what appears as person, place, thing, circumstance, or condition; in the degree that we become nonattached to the things of this world, so that ultimately in some measure we can say, 'I have overcome the world'.[8] In other words, it was as if Jesus had said, 'I can use the things of the world or leave them alone, I can pick up my life or lay it down; I can enjoy good food or get along without it'. In the degree that we learn nonattachment, in that degree, do we attain the Master-consciousness.

Jesus Christ and those like him are a help to us; they are an inspiration—and they are more than that. When we come into the atmosphere of their presence or writings, we automatically are lifted up nearer and nearer to the realization and demonstration of the Master-consciousness.

Actually, the Master-consciousness has appeared on earth in many people, only not to the full degree that it appeared in the person of Jesus Christ. From the effect of this man's life, there is no doubt but that he must have attained it probably to the highest degree ever known, and there probably have been only one or two others who attained that same degree of Master-consciousness. The rest of us can be very well satisfied if we attain enough of It to be able to have dominion over our own individual experience and to be able to be of help to those who come within range of our consciousness.

'I can do all things through Christ which strengtheneth me.'[9] The Christ performs the work; the Christ-presence goes before us to make the crooked places straight. There probably is not a metaphysical practitioner in the world who has not felt that sense of the Presence at some time in his healing work, that transcendental experience in which he has felt the *click* of this Super-consciousness, this Master-consciousness, this sense of reality in which he has beheld the spiritual creation, even if only for one second.

Spiritual freedom then is a freedom that comes from Grace. It does not come from taking thought; it does not come through mental effort, although the taking of thought and the mental effort may lift us to a place where we can realize that freedom. 'For my thoughts are not your thoughts, neither are your ways my ways, said the Lord."[10] So none of our thoughts give us our spiritual freedom, even though right thinking may lift us to the place where God's thoughts come through.

But how is this consciousness obtained? How do we attain this spiritual freedom? One way is through contact with someone who has attained some measure of it, or turning to such spiritual literature as will reveal the way of liberation.

But there is another way that will make us independent of all outside aid. It lies in the development of a listening attitude. If, from the minute we awaken in the morning until we are asleep at night, we can practise the 'listening ear', we will arrive. Opening consciousness for the inflow of the Spirit is the highest way known. It will not flow into us from outside somewhere. Rather, it will flow from within to the without. From the depths and the reality of our being comes this flow, and we touch that reality when we learn to close our eyes and open our ears, when we listen to the thoughts that will make us receptive to the great infinite Power within our own being.

Instead of living in bondage to the world of thoughts and things, be *free* !

[10] Isaiah 55 : 8.

CHAPTER XIII

SOLVING INDIVIDUAL PROBLEMS

WITHOUT a knowledge and understanding of God there is no spiritual message, there is no spiritual mission, and there is no spiritual life.

Throughout the ages, the worship of God as something or someone far off and the worship of a God who must be appealed to, petitioned, or told our needs has prevented us from experiencing the presence and power of God.

Today, we have made a real advance spiritually because we are beginning to understand that God is divine consciousness, life eternal, and even more than this, that God is the life and the consciousness of individual you and me. God is not only principle, Soul, or consciousness, but the consciousness and Soul of each and every one of us, the very Spirit, animating principle, and law of our being.

Unless a person clearly perceives the truth of Jesus' statement, 'I and my Father are one',[1] he will not understand why and how it is that all that the Father has is his. The longer we perpetuate God as something separate and apart from ourselves, the longer will we be seeking to get our allness from a God somewhere outside of us. In proportion, however, as we realize that God is closer to us than breathing, and that Jesus knew what he was talking about when he said, 'The kingdom of God is within you[2] . . . I and my Father are one[3] . . . Son, thou art ever with me, and all that I have is thine',[4] will we understand that all that the Father has is ours.

In that realization, we are able to give up fear. We all know the terrors of fear, so it is natural to ask, 'How can I lose fear? How can I give up my fear?' There is only one way, and that

[1] John 10:30.   [2] Luke 17:21.
[3] John 10:30.   [4] Luke 15:31.

is to know God as the very reality of our being. If we know God to be our life, how then can we fear for our life, for our supply, or for our security? It is our realization of one oneness with God which constitutes our safety and security, our health, longevity, immortality, and eternality.

In no way can we overcome fear as long as we believe that we are separated from God. But not even fear in the form of an atomic bomb, a war, a germ, or some such thing as an economic depression will enter our consciousness after we have learned first, that God is life eternal, second, that the mind that was in Christ Jesus is our mind, and third, that the very place whereon we stand is holy ground:

God is here where I am. We are not two separate beings in two separate places, one trying to contact the other; but right here where I stand, God is.

God is the great I, the great I AM. Therefore, God is all there is of my being. God is the mind of me, the Soul of me, and the life of me. God is the Spirit of me, the law and principle of me; and wherever God is, I am, for we are one and not two.

In that realization, there is nothing to be feared.

If this is true, why do we have discords? Why do we have sins and fears? Why do we have wars, unemployment, and catastrophes? The answer is that these problems are caused by the belief that human beings are separate and apart from God. They do not consciously realize their oneness with God, and they have not learned to apply and utilize the truth of being in their experience.

As we learn to live consciously in the presence of God and to realize God as the only Power, it becomes unnecessary to take thought for our life. But until the day when all this becomes so much a part of our consciousness that we need no longer consciously think of it, it is wise to have some knowledge of how to go about bringing the presence and power of God into our actual, individual, daily experience.

When we are asked for help, in this approach, we drop all thought of the person who turns to us for help; we drop all thought of the nature of the claim and turn to the word God. Our treatment begins with God and ends with God. We make God the first word of the treatment; we begin with God; and we proceed from God somewhat in this manner:

God is life eternal; God is incorporeal and spiritual; and God contains within Itself no trace of matter, no trace of materiality, no trace of carnality, and no trace of mortality. God is infinite Spirit, the divine Life of the individual—whether that individual is patient or practitioner. God is the life of all being, and that Life is wholly spiritual and is without organs and functions. That Life is the perfect expression of Its own being.

This is not a formula, nor is it to be used as such. Formulas are not effective in the spiritual realm. This is merely an example of the application of the principle.

In this treatment, we have not come down for a single moment from God and Its manifestation of Its own being. And what is this God about whom we have declared this? God is the life of you and the life of me, the mind of you and the mind of me. God is the Soul and the Spirit and the substance and the body of you and of me. Therefore, even in staying up with God, we have not separated the patient from God, or God from His own infinite expression—His own child, from whatever we see as the individualization of God's being.

Now let us suppose someone has called and said, 'I am ill. Will you give me help?' The answer from the practitioner is, 'Certainly, I will give you help immediately.' Notice right there that we use the word 'I'. Does that mean that the practitioner will give the help? No, he may have voiced that, but that is not what he meant. He meant what he said: 'I will give you help,' but the *I* he is talking about is God. We always begin with God—not with patient and not with practitioner. We go out from God: 'I, God, will give you help immediately.'

In another case, we may be asked to help someone who is the victim of alcoholism or someone who is unemployed. Immediately, the answer comes back: 'I am helping you; I will be with you'; 'I will help at once'; or, 'I will give a treatment at once.' Again we begin with I, and I is God. There is only one I, so therefore, the I which is the practitioner is God, but the I, which is the patient is also God. Inasmuch as we are dealing with only one I, can that I be something separate and apart from Its own activity? Is it impossible to separate God from the activity of Its own being?

God cannot enter the realm of unemployment, of sin or sinful habits, or even of the fear of death. God is infinite being, and God is infinitely and individually expressing Itself as the Consciousness of the universe, as the Life, the Soul, and the Spirit of the universe. God is expressing Itself as the infinity of Being, and, because God is infinite, God is infinite in expression, infinite in form and variety, but yet always God.

There is no room in this spiritual universe for anything less than God—God expressing Itself, God manifesting Itself, God individualizing Itself, God showing Itself forth as individual being, your individual being and mine—but always God.

Being infinite individuality, God must appear as individual you and me, as individual 'he' and 'she', and as individual it—but it is always God appearing; it is always God expressing; it is always God, God, God. We are never expressing God: God is expressing Its own infinite being and is expressing that infinite Being in infinite form and variety, in infinite individuality, in harmony and grace and beauty. Always God is doing all of that.

The treatment is always up here with God. We do not bring God down to the human scene and attempt to make a human being better. We learn to disregard the human being and become more and more acquainted with the divine Being. Someone may ask, 'What connection has that with a patient, and how can that have any bearing on the one asking for help?' It doesn't! Who wants it to? We are not interested in seeing a sick mortal become a well mortal, or an unemployed human being become an employed human being, or a sinning mortal become reformed. That is not what our interest is. We are interested in seeing God disclose, unfold, and reveal Itself. All we are interested in is *seeing* God—God appearing here and God appearing there, God appearing as infinite activity, infinite individuality, infinite personality, but always God *appearing*!

We do not connect God with anybody called a patient. God itself could not do that. If God could connect Itself to a human being, there would not be a sick human being in the world. It is only because God takes no cognizance of human beings that it is possible for a human being to get sick.

A human being is a part of what has been termed the mortal sense to which Jesus referred when he said, 'My kingdom is not of this world'.[5] And because he knew that his kingdom was not of this world, he would not permit himself to be crowned, nor to be made the head of an army designed to lead the Hebrews to freedom. He loved those Hebrews, he loved the people of his own church, of his own race, and of his own circle; but he would not permit himself to go out and perform any temporal deed. His mission was a spiritual mission and his universe, a spiritual one. He was satisfied for God alone to be Good, and even said of himself, 'Why callest thou me good? there is none good but one, that is, God.'[6]

No one who follows the teaching of Jesus would ever want his patients or students to look at him and say, 'You are good'; or, 'You have God's goodness!' No, he wants them to look within their own being and find the kingdom of God within them, find God as the very centre of their being, as the Consciousness, Soul, Life, and Spirit of them, and then all their human characteristics will drop away.

They will not die: They will make a transition from the mortal sense of existence to the spiritual while they remain right here enjoying good food, beautiful scenery, satisfying companionships, and every experience that is part of this human existence, only they will learn that it is not human existence and that there is not a good side and a bad side to it. Eventually, they will learn that what they have been calling a human existence is really the divine spiritual existence and that it has in it no sickness or health, no poverty or wealth. It is all God's own being pouring forth and expressing Itself in so many ways and so many forms and so many varieties that they can hardly keep up with the beauty of it and the joy of it.

[5] John 18:36.   [6] Matthew 19:17.

In this work, we not only begin our treatment with the word God, but we also forget the name and identity of the individual who asks for help, as well as the name of the disease. As a matter of fact seventy-five per cent of the time, we are giving a condition the name of a disease that is not there. Even *materia medica* cannot diagnose all of its cases correctly. Calling a disease by name is nonsense because we do not know the name of the disease, and even if we should go to a hospital for a diagnosis, we have no assurance that we will be given the right name for it. Why be concerned about whether we can name a disease or are familiar with the physiology of the body? I have never yet met a metaphysician, except those few who have come out of *materia medica*, who knew anything about human anatomy.

When the patient reports that his pain is very severe in a certain spot, the metaphysician has no way of knowing what it is, whether it is the heart that is troubling him or an accumulation of gas, or some other problem. Why burden the practitioner with detailed information as to where the difficulty seems to be when all the practitioner is called upon to know is that God is the life of this universe, and that God is the law, the principle, and the being of this entire universe, whether the universe appears as man, woman, child, animal, or plant. God is the life of all being!

The commonest mistake made in metaphysical practice is in looking at some sick or sinful being and saying, 'You are God's perfect child!' What nonsense! With our eyes we can never see any part of God's creation. All that we can see with our eyes and hear with our ears is a mortal dream, a false concept of reality, a human concept, that which has been called the 'Adam-man', 'fallen man', or the 'Adam-dream'. All these terms make up the grand and glorious nothingness of mortal creation. To look at anything we can see, regardless of how beautiful it may be, and call it spiritual is to lose the whole demonstration of the spiritual life.

In the human scene, there are probably few things more beautiful to look upon than a towering mountain, a gentle valley or babbling stream, a well-proportioned human form, a piece of sculpture, or a masterpiece of painting. But regardless of how beautiful it is, it is not spiritual. To look at it and call it spiritual is nonsense and will not bring forth spiritual demonstration.

Spiritual demonstration grows out of the ability to begin with the word God and from there to go on to God as Life, Love, and divine Wisdom, and to see God manifesting, expressing, revealing, disclosing and unfolding Its own being in all of Its infinite beauty, intelligence, permanence, and grandeur. Since God is infinite, there is nothing else but God. All that is expressing harmony and peace and joy is God.

We cannot have God and something else; therefore, there is only God. It is only God that is unfolding and disclosing Itself as individual you and me. But even when It is individual you and me, It is still God disclosing Its own being, manifesting and expressing Its own being in all Its health and all of Its permanence, and in all Its glory.

That is treatment! After a while when it becomes such second nature to begin with the word God that we do not have to think about it any more, then we just look out on the universe and all we can see is God showing Itself forth. We do not see the human scene. We really do not. Even when in our practice we are dealing with sick and sinning human beings, coming in and out of our office, we really are not aware of them as being human. All we are aware of is that little glimpse we get from the eyes which is the Soul shining through, and that Soul is God.

There is only one thing that brings forth a feeling of closer kinship with some than with others, and that is when a student or patient gives some indication that what he is seeking is God and the mysteries of God rather than healing alone. Those who continuously cry about their little problems as if they were the most important issues of life, instead of merely stating what they are and saying, 'Show me the principle of healing', are usually the ones who claim that a practitioner is partial and wonder why he gives so much time to one and so little to another.

These people as a rule do not appreciate the fact that the

practitioner or teacher on the spiritual path who has attained some measure of the understanding and love of God cannot spend too much time talking about the problems of humanity. To a practitioner, problems merely provide an opportunity to bring forth the principle of God so when one patient is apparently given more time than another, it is perhaps because the one getting that attention is the one more eager for the unfoldment and revelation of God. He brings his problem into the discussion only as a basis from which to work, as an 'excuse' to get on to the subject of God.

Problems at a particular stage of development are more or less necessary because few people would seek God without some deep problem to be solved. While our problems may be stepping stones, we must not let them become our whole existence, but rather use them as the excuse to arrive at an understanding of our relationship to God and of how to utilize this understanding to work them out.

Spiritual truth or treatment is not used to change a material circumstance or to make a demonstration of materiality. This is a vitally important point in the practice of The Infinite way and almost startling, especially when it is remembered how some of us in the past have tried to demonstrate a parking space down the street, a new automobile, a hat, or a dress. Not that we are not entitled to the parking space, the automobile, the hat, or the dress. We are entitled to it on the highest level of demonstration obtainable, but only as an *added thing*, only as a result of seeking the kingdom of God and finding It. We are not entitled to go to God and say, 'I need a new pair of shoes, and money with which to meet my rent.' We do have the right to go to God and find in God spiritual wholeness and let God interpret that to us as shoes, rent, a parking space, an automobile, books to be published, or anything else.

If we let our human picture unfold itself of its own accord through the development of our spiritual consciousness so that all of our good humanhood becomes an added thing, we shall be living and working and having our being in accord with the law of God. If we let ourselves be tempted to use this truth to demonstrate a loaf of bread, we will not make our spiritual demonstration. Such demonstration as we make will merely be on the mortal, material, or mental level, and it will not lead to our spiritual development and unfoldment.

It probably is necessary for some students to go through the mental stages of metaphysical work. I am in no position to know or to judge because I have never been able to understand the mental approach and have not been able to use affirmations or denials, so I do not know whether or not they are necessary at any stage of unfoldment. I am certainly ready to admit that those stages may be necessary, but in admitting that, I would go only so far as to say that these are necessary merely as steps leading from the material to the mental, and further up into the spiritual.

The Master wisely said, 'My sheep hear my voice'.[7] Every earnest seeker who prays for guidance will be led to his teaching and to those teachers who can meet him on his level of consciousness. No one should ever permit himself to be drawn to anyone except such a one as can meet his spiritual need, one who has the particular bread that is for him. Every person must be the judge for himself of what is good for him, so only those who are attracted by the particular state of consciousness represented in this book can understand and receive and respond to this message.

You might come in contact with a thousand teachers, and nine hundred and ninety-nine of them would have nothing to offer you. There is only one who is meant for you—not that they are not good, those others, but they are good only for the person for whom they are meant. For you, there will be only one or two along life's pathway who will meet your particular state of consciousness. You may get a grain of truth from each one, but when it comes to your real teacher or teaching, there is only one of those.

In my whole life, only one state of thought has registered with me: 'I and my Father are one . . . Son, thou art ever with me, and all that I have is thine . . . The place whereon

[7] John 10:27.

thou standest is holy ground . . . Take no thought for your life
. . . Not by might, nor by power, but by my spirit.' That meets
with a response in my consciousness. That is my teacher—not
a man, woman, or a book. My teacher is my own state of consciousness of oneness. That is my teacher regardless of who
voices it, and anyone with that state of consciousness will
always find in me a real state of receptivity.

Try to remember that your teacher is your state of consciousness expressing itself in infinite ways of spiritual impartation.
That is your teacher, but whether you find it in my books or
someone else's makes no difference. Stick to the particular
teaching which brings out a response in you, but do not try
to mix a great many different teachings.

To everyone else, I say very, very honestly: Find your
teacher. Do not make the mistake of following a teacher or a
teaching because your friends and relatives follow him or it.
Your demonstration is to go to the kingdom of God within
your own being and to pray that you be shown your teacher
and your teaching. Then be fair with it: Stay with it: follow
it. If the time ever comes when you outgrow it, be satisfied and
willing to outgrow it, but stay with that which God has revealed to you until God reveals another step.

Keep your thoughts high, and you will find it easy then for
your human experience to unfold harmoniously. Do not let
your demonstration come through 'hard work', but rather
through a natural spiritualization of thought, through developing your consciousness on higher and higher spiritual
levels. Have always at hand a word, a sentence, or a paragraph
of spiritual wisdom to help keep thought on a high plane.

The willingness to have God revealed as your consciousness,
to voice truth as you understand it, to discipline yourself to
complete reliance on the Within, to overcome your hate, fear,
or love the world of effect—these lead to God's expressing
Itself as your individual being. God-consciousness realized
follows a dedication to the word and works of God.

CHAPTER XIV

GOD IS NOT MOCKED

THE real purpose of spiritual teaching is not merely to show students how to make the demonstration of daily living and daily harmony, nor even the demonstration of peace and health in a human way. There is something more important in life than making the organs of the body a little healthier, or prolonging physical life a few years, or increasing a person's income by ten or even a thousand dollars a week.

The real import of The Infinite Way is that we realize that life is Spirit and therefore our individual expression of that life must be spiritual and our entire existence show forth the harmonies and perfections of Spirit, and not merely physical health and wealth.

Be not deceived; God is not mocked: for whatsoever a man soweth, that shall he also reap.

For he that soweth to his flesh shall of the flesh reap corruption; but he that soweth to the Spirit shall of the Spirit reap life everlasting.

Galatians 6:7, 8.

'Be not deceived; God is not mocked.' Judging the world from the evidence of the five physical senses, we would have to admit that God is mocked. Surely, God never planned for Its creation any such scenes or experiences as we witness in the human world, and so, judging by human experience and from what we see about us of sin, disease, wars, and depressions, it is practically impossible to believe that God is not mocked.

'For I have no pleasure in the death of him that dieth.'[1] How can we reconcile that statement with the statistical fact that

[1] Ezekiel 18:32.

not only are our highways filled with death every day, but that we send the flower of our youth off to war to make sure they get killed even faster than would be the normal incidence in traffic accidents? Yes, in the human scene, God is mocked.

Anyone who has ever spent any amount of time in healing work—spiritual, mental, or medical—or with those suffering from cancer or tuberculosis would certainly be tempted to agree that God is mocked. Yet Scripture says that God is not mocked. It also says that as we sow, so shall we reap. If we sow to the flesh, we shall reap of the flesh; if we sow to the Spirit, we shall reap of the Spirit. In this passage is the answer to the whole problem of sin, disease, and death.

God is not mocked while we are sowing to the Spirit, living the life of the Spirit, in attunement or at-one-ment with God, with our thought on the spiritual way of living, the spiritual pleasures of life, and the spiritual business and activity of life. Then God is not mocked, in that those who sow to the Spirit reap spiritual treasure.

In the same way, God is not mocked when we turn *from* God, that is, when we turn away from the spiritual way of living. Then we pay the penalty for that desertion, and in that also God is not mocked since it is not possible to reap the good of God while violating the laws of God.

Reaping the result tomorrow of our acts of today or reaping the results of any of our former acts at a later time is known in Oriental teachings as karma and in philosophy as cause and effect. In scriptural language, it is the law of 'whatsoever a man soweth, that shall he also reap'.

This makes it appear as if we could experience both good and evil, choose to do good and receive good, or choose to do evil and reap evil. However, ancient Scripture, as well as the more modern biblical and metaphysical teachings, reveals that the spiritual life is the only real life, and therefore the only cause being God or Spirit, the only effect is spiritual—good. This means that as long as we live in accord with the principle of Spirit, which is our original and only real existence, we reap the fruitage of that harmonious and perfect existence. At some point or other in our evolving state of consciousness, however, there sprang up a sense of an existence apart from God, and we came to believe that we were something separate from God.

As long as we accept a material code of life, as long as we accept the concept of finiteness and limitation, we reap that very state of existence, although actually in belief only; whereas by turning and re-turning to our original state of spiritual existence, we become aligned with all that is good, spiritual, and harmonious.

Many people who have had the benefit of metaphysical help in any of its various schools, and then later found that they were not receiving healings, have learned that what they were trying to do was to bring the law of Spirit, or God, into their mortal or material sense of existence. In other words, they were trying to patch up what has been called this 'Adam-dream', trying to improve a mortal concept of life, instead of turning from the mortal and the material to the spiritual life.

But how are we to know that we are sowing to the fleshly existence, and how can we turn from it to the spiritual sense of life? From our very birth, all of us have been living in a material sense of existence, an existence made up of catering to the personal 'I', trying to earn a living for the 'I', trying to gain something, acquire something, or achieve something. All that is the limited or finite sense of existence. That is what we were born into as human beings and that is what we now must turn away from in order to sow to the Spirit.

The spiritual sense of life which is the direct opposite of the human sense of life is based on the premise that 'I and my Father are one',[2] that all that the Father has is ours, and therefore, instead of our having to demonstrate, get, or achieve health, harmony, success, and wealth, we become that point in consciousness through which God manifests Itself to the world. This is how we sow to the Spirit and reap the Spirit.

God is not mocked. God, the omnipresent Reality of our being, the all-knowing, ever-present Consciousness, ever aware of our existence, certainly is not mocked, because we cannot violate the laws of God and avoid the results of that violation. Setting oneself up as a person who deserves something, is

[2] John 10:30.

worthy of something, or is of himself something is sowing to the finite, limited sense, and therefore reaping corruption, a reaping which may take the form of living well in the prosperous or boom days and living poorly in depressions, of being healthy in our youth and then beginning to deteriorate in our middle years.

All of that is dissolved as soon as we begin to realize that we have no demonstration to make, that God is the only one who has a demonstration to make, and that God's demonstration consists of expressing Itself as individual you and me. The moment we drop the responsibility from our own being, put the government on His shoulder, and realize that God is our life and our Soul, and that the responsibility for our success or failure and for our work in life is on the shoulder of the Principle that brought us into manifestation—that moment we begin to live the spiritual life.

This can be done very quickly, or it can take a long time, depending on how tenacious we are in our determination to perpetuate the 'I' that is Joel or Bill or Mary, how determined we are to have our own way in this life. It is true that those who live to that personal sense of existence oftentimes achieve what they are seeking—personal health, success, and wealth—but in most cases it proves to be Dead Sea fruit, because after it has been achieved it is discovered that this is not it. Those who turn to the spiritual sense of existence somehow seem to have found happiness, peace, and security, and yet to have achieved them without doing so at someone else's expense.

In this age, it is possible to duplicate the miracles of the Master in feeding and healing the multitudes, but only when we begin to work, not from the standpoint of our personal powers or our personal wealth, but from the infinity and omnipresence of God.

God is a word that has many meanings. It means many things to many people, and each one must determine for himself what God is to him. Let us for a moment agree, however, that God is the creative principle of the universe, the infinite wisdom of the universe, and the great law. Is it not possible then to see that this Law, this Infinity, can pour Itself through you or through me in the same manner that It poured Itself through the Master? Actually, It appears *as* you and *as* me.

There is only one Law; there is only one Principle; but instead of our attempting to use that Law it remains for each one of us to permit that Law or Principle to use us. That is one of the great differences between the finite sense of life and the infinite. Too often we try to use spiritual Law and infinite Power for some personal good. The Law really works the other way: The Law uses us. Probably in scriptural language that would be something like saying that 'whatsoever ye do, do all to the glory of God'.[3] In other words, we are not doing it at all; God is doing it through us, or as us, for Its own glory.

No one should make the mistake of believing that in healing and feeding multitudes the Master was building up glory for himself. Had his purpose been for the glorification of a man named Jesus, there would have been no principle, no rule, or no law to be made manifest in our individual experience, because with the departure of Jesus there then would have been no one to show forth or use this law. On the contrary, the Master told his disciples, 'If I go not away, the Comforter will not come unto you'.[4] In other words, if we persist in turning to this person called Jesus or in believing that there is some personal power that you or I have which we can use for our own good, we shall never learn the principle or be able to experience its good in our lives.

If anyone today believes for a moment that truth is for the purpose of glorifying or showing forth the great powers or saintliness of any individual, he is entirely missing the mark. The whole purpose of spiritual truth is to show forth the great principle that God is the universal life and the universal power, that God is ever available, and that God is here for the manifestation of Its own power and Its own glory.

That certainly eliminates you and me as people with personal healing powers, or enriching powers. There is no such person on earth—not you, not me, nor anyone else—and there never has been. The only Power is God manifested *as* individual

---

[3] I Corinthians 10:31.   [4] John 16:7.

being, and then manifested only through the understanding of this divine idea.

In the degree that we are able to open our consciousness and let the divine Consciousness take possession of us, in that degree do we show forth the harmony, health, joy, and peace which is of God and not of man. The moment we realize that God, this great divine I is really the I that I am, we have begun to see the universality of God. When we have stopped thinking out upon life from the finite sense of ourselves as human beings, subject to all the mortal and material laws, and have begun to realize that the I of me is God, the I, the infinite consciousness, is God, in that moment we have lost the finiteness, we have lost the sense of separateness from God that has driven us out into the world as prodigals, and we have begun to retrace our steps back to the Father's house, there to be vested with the purple robe and the jewelled ring.

Brethren, if a man be overtaken in a fault, ye which are spiritual, restore such an one in the Spirit of meekness . . .

Bear ye one another's burdens, and so fulfil the law of Christ.

For if a man think himself to be something, when he is nothing, he deceiveth himself.

Galatians 6 : 1-3.

We spiritualize our consciousness when we can realize even in a measure the truth that God is the creative source, principle, and life of our being, and then share that understanding by beginning to know the truth about everyone in the universe. We bear our neighbour's burden, not by paying his rent for him, nor by sitting and sympathizing with him in his illness. We bear his burden, and actually we bear it away from him as we realize the spiritual nature of individual being and begin to share that with our neighbour in the understanding that we are all children of the one father, all offspring of the same Spirit, and whatever is a law unto one must be the law unto all spiritual being.

Let him that is taught in the word communicate unto him that teacheth in all good things.

As we have therefore opportunity, let us do good unto all men, especially unto them who are of the household of faith.

Galatians 6:6,10.

Many of us may think of that as meaning that we should help only those who are of our faith—of our church or our spiritual or metaphysical teaching—and we probably have learned to leave everybody else strictly alone. This will not do. While we do not go about preaching the Gospel in the sense of proselyting or of forcing metaphysics or the spiritual life on those who for some reason are not ready for it or desirous of it, at least not in the way we wish to present it, nevertheless, it becomes our duty the moment we realize one iota of spiritual truth to know that it is the truth about all of God's creation, and therefore to leave no man outside.

It is true that we can go a step further with those who are of the household of faith. Wherever an individual shows an interest in a spiritual teaching, we can go so far as to talk to him about it, offer him books or pamphlets, or give him individual healing help—all depending on his readiness to receive it. Naturally, we can go further with those who show an interest in our particular teaching, but that does not absolve us from our major duty of realizing God as the universal Principle, and leaving no one outside of Its fold.

In the First Commandment, 'Thou shalt have no other Gods before me',[5] is found the entire secret of demonstration—the realization of God as the one and only Power. If we understand God as Truth and realize that this Truth which is God is the I AM of your being and of mine and of all being, then that Truth will not be mocked. Then we will not be dragged through sin, disease, lack, and limitation, and if these temptations do come nigh unto us, they will be quickly and easily removed.

God, Truth, is not mocked. If we abide in this truth of our being, if we begin to accept for ourselves the fact that God is

[5] Exodus 20:3.

the one and only power and that this God is our life and our very consciousness, then we have the ever presence and availability of eternal life and eternal and infinite supply. Truth, then, is really not mocked. Through Grace, we show forth in a measure the infinite harmony of God—not by taking thought, but through Grace!

Of my own self I am nothing; of my own self I can do nothing; but the infinite nature and character of God, the infinite Allness which is God, is forever pouring Itself through as my individual being, ever appearing here on earth as my individual being, the Word made flesh. I can meet any and every demand made upon me, not as if I were of myself something, but because the infinity of God pours through as all those who turn to It.

With such realization, we begin to experience that peace of mind and that security which are of God, and we experience these in even greater degree the moment we fulfil the Second Commandment, 'Love thy neighbour as thyself',[6] so well exemplified in the sixth chapter of Galatians.

To love our neighbour as ourselves means, first of all, to recognize God as the universal Principle and realize that whatever we have declared of our own being is the truth of every man's being, whether or not he knows it, realizes it, or is demonstrating it. To love our neighbour means to un-see him as male or female, as white or black, as Jew or Gentile, as German, Japanese, Russian, American, or British, and to see through that exterior to the life which is God, to the mind and the Soul which is God.

We are living today in an age when anything can happen, an age of uncertainty, unrest, and danger. If there is any hope for the world, that hope will have to come through those who have attained spiritual illumination. It is not going to come through any human documents or doctrine. It is not going to come through an atomic bomb or any kind of a pact—Atlantic or Pacific. How can it? All those things mean death and

[6] Mark 12 : 31.

destruction not only to a so-called enemy, but, as we have seen, any defence is a double-edged sword, and 'all they that take the sword shall perish with the sword'.[7]

History is replete with accounts of the downfall and resurgence of nation after nation. One after another has disappeared, has been defeated and gone down in spite of its many victories on the field of battle. If anyone believes that a combination of Western powers or the possession of the atomic bomb is going to guarantee peace, he has failed to read the lesson of history, and moreover he knows even less about spiritual truth.

The only way in which peace is going to come to the world is through the illumined consciousness of those individuals who turn to the Spirit for Its fruitage. Somewhere, sometime, this spiritual evolution will begin. Probably the first public statement about this, or at least the most widely known public statement about it, came from Steinmetz, the electrical wizard, who left as one of his last messages to the world his conviction that in this age spiritual power would come to the fore and be recognized as the great power and that more advances in spiritual knowledge would be made in this age than had ever been attained before.

There may or may not be another war. Who can prophesy in regard to the human picture? There may even be found a way of ending a threatened war by human means, but at best it will be a temporary thing since, judging by the history of the past, wars have been going on since the beginning of recorded time, and there is no indication that they have come or will come to an end.

There is one hope, however, and that is that at no time in the world's history has spiritual awareness been manifest among men as it is today. True, at all periods in the world's history, there have been men in the priesthood and in the ministry who have known spiritual power, who have known their true identity, and who have been able to bring this spiritual power into concrete manifestation for themselves and for others. The situation is somewhat different now, however, because today throughout the world there are people like you

[7] Matthew 26:52.

and me, average people, who have gained some little glimpse of what spiritual power can do, and who have had some proof of the power of the Spirit—healing either of the body, of the mind, of the purse, or of morals.

The time has now come for you and me and for everyone who has any awareness of truth to accept the responsibility of thinking in universal terms, of beginning to know that God is not mocked even on a national or international scale, and that the law of God does operate universally.

We who individually accept this great revelation of Christianity, that is, of the omnipotence and omnipresence of the Spirit of God in man, must each and every day recognize that this Christ is present wherever an individual raises his thought to God. And today, all over the world people are lifting their thoughts to invoke help from God. It is true that some of them are thinking of this God as a Gentleman up on a cloud; others are thinking of this God as Jesus Christ of Nazareth, and still others are thinking of God in some different form. What their idea of God is, however, is not important since, whatever it is, it is only a concept. Everyone has his own concept of God, and yet there have been few in all the history of the world who have known God and what God is. But those who have achieved the actual awareness of God have come to see this truth: *I am He.*

Regardless of one's concept of God, those who believe in God have this in common: They believe that God is present and that He is available as a help in whatever the emergency may be. Soldiers at the front and others in times of danger or in dire need have lifted their thoughts to God, and whether the God to which they prayed was a Hebrew God, a Methodist or a Catholic One, when they turned their thought to Him, they found immediate help.

It is the person who is living the spiritual life who can make that experience a more universal one. In other words, every time we consciously realize the Christ as an ever present principle of Light and Life and as an ever present Help wherever an individual raises his thought to God, we make the Christ-truth available to individuals somewhere on earth. We do not know what person in that minute may be lifting himself into this realization of God and finding himself tuned in on our beam. It would not be too important if that merely resulted in saving his individual sense of life or in bringing some personal benefit to him, but the real benefit is that, as we make the Christ available to all those on earth who turn their thought to any concept of God, we bring the universality of the Christ into manifestation and the day nearer when the Christ will be present at the bargaining and the business tables of the world.

The omnipresence of this Christ-power has been proved time after time by men in conferences with labour leaders and management. Many men have proved this Presence in the banking house and the business house, but it takes the recognition of It to bring It into concrete manifestation. Usually, it takes the realization of someone on the spiritual path, one so completely loving his neighbour as himself as to be willing at some part of each day to realize the Christ as omnipresent wherever men lift their thoughts to God.

At every metaphysical lecture in almost any branch of truth, there is usually somebody and often there are groups of people realizing the Presence of the healing Christ, and the result of that is that at most metaphysical lectures and services someone goes away healed of either sin, disease, lack, or limitation. The impersonal realization of the omnipresence of God has freed someone in that audience. Sometimes, the lecturer alone carries the responsibility for that work of spiritual realization, or, on the other hand, committees may be appointed to help in that work. As a matter of fact, every metaphysician every day of the week should be realizing the omnipresence of the Christ wherever men gather on earth—in gambling dives, in prisons, in hospitals, and everywhere else on earth.

If we love our neighbour as ourselves, we will make the effort to realize the Christ—the Christ-presence, the Christ-power—at any place and at any time that any individual anywhere reaches out for the hand of God. 'The Lord's hand is not shortened, that it cannot save.'[8]

But if the hand of God 'is not shortened, that it cannot save',

[8] Isaiah 59:1.

why then are these disasters in the world? It is not because God is not omnipresent, but because the omnipresence of God has not been realized. God is present as your consciousness and mine, as the very activity of your being and mine, but it takes your recognition and mine to bring It into conscious awareness. That is the secret of spiritual healing.

When a practitioner receives a call for help, he realizes God as Life, as Consciousness, as Soul, and God as the Substance of the body, as what appears as the organs and functions of body, as the Wisdom of being, and even as the patient's receptivity to truth.

All the practitioner does is to realize the omnipresence and omnipotence of the Christ in the patient's experience. Is it not but one more step to realize the Christ as omnipresent and omnipotent in the experience of every individual on earth, and therefore to make It available to all those who reach out? No one has a monopoly on God and the Christ. True, there was a time when the Christ was preached only to the Hebrews, but Paul ended that for his particular time when he made the Christ-truth available to all men, and indicated that it was not necessary to become a Hebrew before becoming a Christian.

Today, we must realize that we do not have to become Truth-students in order that God and the Christ be available to us. Let us understand once and for all that metaphysicians are not the only ones who enjoy the benefits of the grace of God. Let us learn to love our neighbour as ourselves, and those of the 'household of faith',[9] but let us not confine it to those of our own household. Let us realize the Christ—the universal Principle, the divine Love—ever available through Grace, not through taking thought, not by learning metaphysics, and not by making affirmations and denials. Wherever a person is and whatever concept of God he accepts and to which he lifts himself, let him there find Grace; let him there find the 'peace of God, which passeth all understanding',[10] because of your and my realization of Omnipresence.

That must be our contribution to the world. We cannot go out into the world and say to it: 'Let's give up war.' We have

[9] Galatians 6:10.   [10] Philippians 4:7.

not yet proved in our own experience that we ourselves can give up individual warfare to a great enough degree to warrant our telling the world to give up its reliance on war as a means of settling international disputes. The time for us to go out and proclaim to the world, 'Let's not have any more wars; let's abide by the teachings of the Master,' will be when we have learned to pay all our bills without being sued and to settle all the problems of our human existence without quarrels.

But until that day comes, we do not have to sit idly by watching the world destroy itself. Oh, no! Just as one individual in Galilee gave forth this teaching for the entire Western world, and left it here intact for all those to accept who will, so we today can repeat that teaching, we can reinstate it in our individual experience and show forth the fruitage of it in our daily living. We ourselves can live by Grace, or at least we can make a beginning. We can pray daily. We can pray without ceasing, and we can make our prayer the realization of spiritual existence. We can begin first of all by realizing that instead of a person's having to be at the standpoint of receiving good, he is at the standpoint of expressing good, sharing good, and bestowing good—not in and of himself, but by the Grace of God, which is the law and the life of his being. In other words, when you and I begin to reverse ourselves, instead of using Truth for some benefit for ourselves, we let Truth *use us* so that It becomes visible as us—God Itself made visible, the Word made flesh.

This is not an easy thing to do, but it is necessary to achieve and accomplish this reversal of our position, whether easy or difficult. The Master set before us no easy task. He said, 'Strait is the gate, and narrow is the way, which leadeth unto life, and few there be that find it'.[11] Indeed, there are few! Most of us still want to use God to improve some human situation in our experience instead of coming to that place in consciousness where we pray:

'*Speak, Lord; for thy servant heareth.*'[12] *Use me; let me be that place in consciousness through which God flows to all*

[11] Matthew 7:14.   [12] I Samuel 3:9.

K

*those seeking God—not seeking my personal power, but
seeking God. Let me be the vehicle or the avenue as which
God pours Itself into expression for all men to receive, until
they themselves learn that all that I am, they are too. All
that Christ is, I am—I in God, and God in me, all one,
children of God; and if children, heirs; and if heirs, joint-heirs
with Christ in God.*

In this way, we break through the personal sense that is so
willing to do for one and not for another. When once we see
through that human frame before us and see that God alone is
pouring Itself forth as individual you and me, that is sowing
to the Spirit. When we see one another as human beings, or if
we see ourselves as human beings with demonstrations to make,
we are sowing to the flesh and will ultimately reap the corruption of the flesh.

God is the life, the mind, and the Spirit of individual being.
God is the reality of our being; and all there is to us is God.
When we realize this, we are sowing to the Spirit, beholding
one another as we are, and we must reap spiritually. When we
awaken, we shall see Him as He is. We do not have to die to
awaken; we do not have to die to become like Him. We can do
our *dying* right here and now, and we do, if only a little bit of
our humanhood drops off each day, if in only a small way we
realize that we have no demonstration to make, that we do not
have to take thought as to what we shall eat or what we shall
drink or wherewithal we shall be clothed. All we have to do is
to relax and to realize that the heavenly Father, which is right
here and now, knows that we have need of all these things,
and that it is His good pleasure to give us the Kingdom.

At the moment we relax our conscious thinking in the sense
of dropping responsibilities and actually accepting the truth
that God knows our need, our whole life changes. Never again
do we have to take thought; never again do we have to plan or
plot; never again do we have to force ourselves mentally or
physically to achieve some good. Our good appears each day
as it is needed: It appears in the form of money; it appears in
the form of friends, relatives, companions, husband, wife, or

home; it appears in any and every form necessary to our present experience, but it appears without taking thought.

One thing we must watch very carefully, and that is to remember that if our thought is on the demonstration of a thing, a person, or a place, we are sowing to the flesh, we are taking thought for things, and that is a violation of the Christ-teaching. If we have a desire for a person, a place, or a thing—for any form of good—we are violating the Christ-teaching. We are not supposed to take thought for things or persons. Our whole mind must be on God Itself as the Reality of our being, as the infinite Consciousness of our being, and not on the forms as which God appears. In that realization, we drop our human desire for person, place, and thing, and we let them appear to us in their proper order, and it may not be the person, place, or thing we have been thinking about, but it will be a very satisfying one.

In Luke, the Master told his disciples to take no thought for what they should eat or what they should drink or wherewithal they should be clothed, and he called their attention to the lilies of the field and to the birds, summing it all up with: 'Your Father knoweth that ye have need of these things . . . [and] it is your Father's good pleasure to give you the kingdom.'[13] On the day when I realized the meaning of that particular passage, I saw that sowing to the flesh meant trying to achieve something in the manifest realm, even good things like positions, dollars, or companions. I realized that it was on that very point, that is, the attempt on our part to decide what person, place, or thing we desired and then trying to use the law of God to get it, that we wrecked our ship of life.

In that passage, I found the answer to all of life's problem. I saw that as I took no thought for those things, but kept my thought stayed on Him, as I kept my attention centred on God and the things of God, and as I tried to realize within my own being the spiritual nature of life, suddenly I found it was not necessary to take thought about these things of daily living. They always found a way of getting to my table or my desk a little before I knew that I needed them. I still find that that

[13] Luke 12 : 30, 32.

principle works, and it is not necessary for me to think about who is going to do this, or when, or how it is to be accomplished, or why. I find that as long as I abide in this realization of God and then do everything to the best of my ability as it is presented to me to do, that seems to be sufficient for the experience I am having at the present time.

CHAPTER XV

IMMANUEL

Make a joyful noise unto the Lord, all ye lands.

Serve the Lord with gladness: come before his presence with singing.

Know ye that the Lord he is God: it is he that hath made us, and not we ourselves; we are his people, and the sheep of his pasture.

Enter into his gates with thanksgiving, and into his courts with praise: be thankful unto him, and bless his name.

For the Lord is good; his mercy is everlasting; and his truth endureth to all generations.

Psalm 100.

'Know ye that the Lord he is God: it is he that hath made us, and not we ourselves.' Let us take that as our guiding light! let us try to realize in this moment that it is He that has made us, and not we ourselves. Just to be reminded of that truth and keep it uppermost in consciousness should be a healing influence. Immediately, whatever of sin, disease, or discord may be floating about anywhere should begin to fade out with the realization: 'It is he that hath made us, and not we ourselves.' That places the responsibility for our health, wealth, peace, safety, and security upon God, the creative Principle.

To each one of us, God means something different, but those differences are not important. What is important is that we recognize that there is a creative Principle, a causative Power, and that It created us, and not we ourselves.

In the New Testament, John confirms this truth when he says, 'Now are we the sons of God'.[1] Again it is made clear that God is the causative or creative principle of our being. If once we are able to accept that, how comforting it is to realize that that which God has created He must maintain and sustain. God must be the law unto it—not only the law giver, but the law

[1] John 3:2.

itself. God must be the life of that which God creates, and if God is the life of our being, then our being is eternal and immortal. Therefore, to accept even for a moment the belief or fear of death, of passing on, or of leaving this plane of consciousness is really a sin against the Holy Ghost. We must honour God, but we dishonour and disavow God when we forget that 'it is he that hath made us, and not we ourselves'

As the inner meaning of the Bible unfolds and reveals itself to us, the Scriptures play a greater and greater part in our lives and in our work. The Bible is not too important merely as a religious book. Many people may have felt, as I did, that much of it made little sense. It is only since spiritual realization has come that I am able to see that the importance of Scripture does not lie in making affirmations or in quoting Scripture, but in accepting its statements, analysing and pondering them, and receiving from within the real meaning or essence of the Word.

'We are his people, and the sheep of his pasture.' Very early the idea of God as a sheep tender who cares for his flock became embodied in Hebrew literature. That is, of course, only symbolic, but it does help us to see that we are the creation of this great God, and it brings to our thought and awareness this sense of a very loving Principle, a loving Power, and an ever watchful One who cares for and watches over this being and body of ours, even as the sheep tender guards his charges and gives them pasturage. 'It is he that hath made us, and not we ourselves.' We are under His supervision, under the divine guardianship of an infinitely wise and all-loving Principle which we call God, or Father-Mother.

Enter into his gates with thanksgiving, and into his courts with praise: Be thankful unto him, and bless his name.

Psalm 100 : 4.

In all thy ways acknowledge him, and he shall direct thy paths.

Proverbs 3 : 6.

Thou wilt keep him in perfect peace, whose mind is stayed on thee.

Pray without ceasing.   I Thessalonians 5 : 17.

In these and hundreds of other passages, not only of the ancient Hebrews, but from the time of the Master on through the Christian era, is found the teaching of the necessity of acknowledging God in all our ways, acknowledging God as the creative Principle of our own being and the Source of our supply, acknowledging God with praise and with thanksgiving for all the good which we experience in our life. There is no other way to pray without ceasing than to acknowledge continuously this infinite Power and Presence, this great Keeper of the universe and of all His creation which includes the men and women upon the earth.

Human experience from birth to death is nothing more nor less than chance and change. Only the presence of the Christ can transform human experience into spiritual revelation or illumination. If we live without this sense of God's presence, of Christ immanent, then all we have is a physical body beginning to deteriorate almost before we reach thirty years of age, and a continuation of that deterioration until the end.

From the time, however, that the Christ becomes a living reality in consciousness, an ever present awareness, the body becomes that which it originally was intended to be, and that which in reality it is—the temple of the living God. Then there is no such thing as age, change, decomposition, or death—not even passing on, not even transition.

Let us never forget that death itself is a failure. Death is an enemy. True, according to Scripture, it is the last enemy that will be overcome, but it is an enemy, and let no one welcome it, let no one look upon it as a release from human fears or human disease. Death, or passing on, is none of those things. It is a failure to realize our true identity as children of God, 'and if children, then heirs; heirs of God, and joint-heirs with Christ'[2] to all the immortality and eternity of existence.

Does that mean we are to live on this plane for ever? And the answer is: Yes, if we so desire! However, when we leave grammar school for high school or high school for college, it is merely the transition from one state of consciousness to a higher one. And so, if we become aware of our Christhood to

[2] Romans 8:17.

such a degree that we manifest health and strength and vitality in the body, then should the time ever come when a call comes, a realization that there is a higher work to be done, we may leave this plane and go forth into the greater work on higher levels of consciousness.

But let no one for a moment believe that dying out of this body through disease is the way to a greater unfoldment of God-consciousness. It is not true. We may leave this place of existence; we may walk out of this body, or at least appear to walk out of it; we may rise to higher and higher levels of consciousness, since certainly this stratum of consciousness called the earth is not the first or the last; but we do not go from one to the other through failure—and death is failure; death is an enemy, the last enemy.

The way to overcome disease and what the world calls age and decomposition is through the conscious recognition of the great truth of Being. 'For the Lord is good; his mercy is everlasting; and his truth endureth to all generations.' If the Lord, the law of God, or this infinite Christ is good, It cannot for a moment leave us without divine care, protection, and spiritual unfoldment. Since the Lord is good, our experience, even in what we call the human picture, must be good, or else we have taken ourselves out from under the care of this Lord who is good.

'His mercy is everlasting.' Does that permit us, even for one moment, to deteriorate or decompose or die? 'His mercy is everlasting.' It must be just as merciful, just as powerful, and just as loving when we are one hundred years of age as when we are one hundred days of age. Then, is it not our acceptance of a universal belief that would make us believe that God is less merciful and that good is less everlasting because of the passage of what we call time?

'His truth endureth to all generations.' What is His truth? On the understanding of that hinges our entire demonstration of life. What is His truth? It is I AM—I am truth. I am life eternal. I am the resurrection and the life. And this truth which I am is infinite, omnipresent, eternal. There is no separation and no point of division between God and God's truth which I am. Truth is not something that I know; truth is not something that I possess: Truth is something that I am. 'I am the way, the truth, and the life.'[3]

Let us remember this: I am the truth which 'endureth to all generations'. Who said that I am man or woman or child? Who said that? The Master asked that very question: 'Whom do men say that I the Son of man am?'[4] And the foolish answered him saying that he was this man or that man or some reborn one, but that was not the answer. The answer finally came: 'Thou art the Christ, the son of the living God.'[5] Then we are told that Peter did not know that intellectually, but that the Father within, spiritual Consciousness, the divine Wisdom, the spiritual Wisdom of the ages had revealed this truth to the one consciousness prepared to receive it.

We have interpreted Peter's recognition of Jesus as the Christ as applying only to one man in one particular period of time. If that were true, truth would not be everlasting or eternal or throughout all generations. Truth would have stood there on the shores of Galilee for only a brief thirty-three years, or even a briefer three years of spiritual ministry.

Any truth given by the Master must be recognized as universal truth, as being the truth about you and about me, the truth about all who have been on earth or are on earth or who will be on earth unto the end of time. And actually, no one has left the earth, and no one is going to come to earth, since Scripture again tells us that He that came down from heaven and He that went up to heaven are one and the same, always that one and the same I AM: I am the very living truth of God and I am infinite and eternal and omnipresent. I lives throughout all time. 'Lo, I am with you alway, even unto the end of the world.'[6]

This I that we are talking about, which might appear as Joel or Mary, is not a person. It is the presence of God. It is the absolute allness of God, merely appearing as individual you and individual me. It is again the Word made flesh; It is the Word Itself made flesh and dwelling among us as you and as me.

³ John 14:6.   ⁴ Matthew 16:13.
⁵ Matthew 16:16.   ⁶ Matthew 28:20.

Only as we accept this unfoldment and teaching of the Master, will we come into our own heritage of life eternal, and not only ours, but we will bring it forth for all those who are able to accept the truth of the universality of God.

Whether one chooses to continue in the path of the Judaic church and belief, the Christian church and belief, the Hindu or Mohammedan, or whether one chooses to follow any one of the metaphysical movements is of no concern at all in the demonstration of universal truth. Truth is just as available to one as to another, and it is just as available outside the church as in it.

The revelation of man's true identity was never intended to be the property of any one person or of an institution, an organization, or a church. It was meant to be a revelation of the truth of being, and the only purpose or function of any organization is to set forth the universality of that truth, making it available to all who wish or are prepared to receive it.

The universality of truth can no better be seen and understood than through the Immanuel of the Hebrews, the Tao of the Chinese, and the Christ of our Christian era. To me, these words are something like a cloud that I can almost feel behind me, arching itself over my head. Always, I have a sense of that protesting and divine Influence, that Inner Guidance that comes from that cloud around my shoulders—not a cloud in the sense of shutting out, but rather a cloud in the sense of a light foam, something upon which one can lean back and almost feel, as if it were a supporting cloud.

That to me is the meaning of Immanuel, Tao, and the Christ —God-with-me. It is my assurance that I am never alone. It is my conscious awareness of the presence and power of God, a Presence I can sense as It goes before me to make the crooked places straight and to prepare every step of the way for that which is to come.

These three words *Immanuel, Tao,* and the *Christ* all mean the same thing—the presence and power of God with us and in us. They mean the actual realization, the actual feeling of the divine Presence. When the Hebrews spoke of Immanuel, they meant it literally in the sense of a divine Presence with them, not off somewhere, but actually with them. This Immanuel interpreted Itself in human terms as a pillar of cloud by day and a pillar of fire by night, as manna falling from the skies and as water coming from the rock. To the Hebrew prophet, It appeared as food brought by the widow and by the birds. Always, Immanuel, or God with us, appears in a form necessary for us, or to us, at a particular moment.

When Lao-Tze used the word Tao, he meant the Word or the Presence, and always that Word becomes flesh and dwells among us. The word Tao which may be interpreted as the great Infinite Invisible, becomes visible and tangible in the form necessary to your experience and mine—as the health of our body, the wealth of our pocketbook, the happiness of our home, or our security from the dangers of the world.

From the word *Immanuel*, meaning God ever present with us, and the word *Tao*, meaning the self-same thing, we come to the latter-day expression *the Christ*. *The Christ* is the Word, the Infinite Invisible, Tao, or Immanuel, ever present, living with us, and appearing to us as food with which to feed the multitudes where seemingly there is no food, or appearing as the 'peace, be still' to the wild waves of the ocean.

If Christ be not present in your consciousness and mine, then Christianity is a failure and a fraud. If Christ be not present awaiting our recognition, we have no hope in the world. Whether we are in the business world, the religious world, or the world of our home, this Presence is always and ever a guide to us. Wherever we are at this moment, we are because of our readiness for that particular step, but once we have acknowledged the presence of the Christ or felt this Influence in our experience, it may well be that our next step will be a higher one, away from whatever we are doing at the present moment.

The thing for us to remember is that it is not spiritual to desire to be in some other place, or to be doing some other work. That really is an acknowledgment of failure where we are. We are where we are because of our developed or undeveloped state of consciousness, and we will never be in any other place or any other position except through the development and unfoldment of our spiritual consciousness. Therefore, instead of looking back with regret or looking forward wishfully, desirous of being somewhere else and doing something else, let us here and now begin to acknowledge that the place whereon we stand is Holy Ground.

Let there be no misunderstanding about this. If we are not in a good human place, it does not mean that the evil human place is Holy Ground. On the other hand, if we are occupying the very best human place there is on earth, we should not believe that even that is Holy Ground. It has nothing to do with where we humanly appear to be. Holy Ground is that place where we are in divine Consciousness, that place where we recognize ourselves as being the Son of God, the offspring of God, the very I that I am.

When we make the recognition that we are on Holy Ground, we are in spiritual consciousness. Then we need pay no attention to the human place or position we occupy, or even have any sense of achievement if that place happens to be on some spiritual platform, because that is of just as little significance as being on the streetcar conductor's platform in the human scene.

What counts is: Where do we stand spiritually? Where do we stand in consciousness—now? If we stand on the great truth that I am the truth, if we stand in God-consciousness, then we can say that the place whereon we stand is Holy Ground. From that spiritual standpoint, we can accept the truth that all that the Father has is ours, and all that God is, we are.

Moreover, let us not look on anyone humanly, nor permit anyone to look on us humanly to see how close to that divine idea we are. The picture will be very disappointing. Always, we will be dissatisfied with the picture that we see if we look at ourselves or another through finite, human eyes. Always, the great spiritual lights of this and of every age have been criticized and condemned. Every spiritual leader from Moses to the Master was judged, criticized, and condemned from the human standpoint. And who are we to say that in their human experience there may not have been things that could be criticized?

Our function, however, is not to judge according to the appearance or to look at one another humanly to see how far we have come or to what extent we have failed. Our attitude must be that of the spiritual worker who, when he is called to the penitentiary to give help even to a hardened criminal, does not look at that individual and judge from appearances and begin preaching to him, 'If you were just a good human being, what wonderful things God could do through you!' No, he looks right through the human appearance and says: 'Rise, Son of God! Accept your healing in this realization of your true identity, for you are the living Christ. You are the one true son of God.'

It is with this same attitude that a practitioner sits beside the bedside of one who is supposed to be dying. Can the practitioner look at that individual, judge by appearances, and then say: 'Thou art life eternal; thou art the truth of God'? No, only through his developed spiritual sense can the practitioner perceive that what is appearing outwardly as a sick or a sinful human being is actually the very presence of God Itself.

So must we turn our gaze away from what we appear to be humanly and from what our neighbour appears to be and begin with these great and wonderful truths:

The place whereon I stand is Holy Ground; all that the Father has is mine; all that God is, I am.

As we learn to live in that consciousness and to judge only from a spiritual standpoint, then gradually we develop and express that spiritual insight which becomes the light of the world. Then as we go forward in and as that light, everyone within range of our being and within range of our experience feels some degree of attraction towards us, but the attraction is not towards us at all: It is towards the Light which we have become through this great spiritual revelation.

Only in this way are we able to help others in the world and to lift the level of consciousness to the point where some of those touched by this truth begin to perceive their true identity and understand that all that the Father has is theirs unto eternity, forever and forever, without any trace of age or de-composition or disease. In the light of this truth, it is not mortals who understand or achieve health. It is the I that we are, the divine Reality of our being which is the health of our body, the health of our being, and the health of all those who come to us for assistance.

As we begin to realize that health is a property, a quality, and an activity of God, that health is the natural state of eternal life, and that eternal life is the life of your being and of mine, in that degree do we bring forth what appears to the world as bodily health. It appears to the world as a heart that beats so many times per minute, a digestion that is perfect, or an elimination that is satisfactory. It is none of these things. It is really and truly the Christ Itself, the divine harmony and presence of God, visible to the world as harmonious you and harmonious me.

The Lord is my shepherd; I shall not want.

He maketh me to lie down in green pastures; he leadeth me beside the still waters.

He restoreth my soul: he leadeth me in the paths of right-eousness for his name's sake.

Yea, though I walk through the valley of the shadow of death, I will fear no evil: for thou art with me; thy rod and thy staff they comfort me.

Thou preparest a table before me in the presence of mine enemies: thou anointest my head with oil; my cup runneth over.

Surely goodness and mercy shall follow me all the days of my life: and I will dwell in the house of the Lord forever.

Psalm 23.

I will live in the consciousness of God, and if I live in the consciousness of God, I will not only live forever, but I will be divinely and spiritually fed. I will be spiritually guided and governed and directed.

But there is a price, and the price is to live in the consciousness of God, to acknowledge Him in all our ways, to recognize God as the Source and Foundation of our whole existence, to recognize God as the guiding Light, the infinite Wisdom and Intelligence of our being, to trust God to bring forth divine harmony as our individual experience, and to pray without ceasing.

In doing all this, we are being obedient to the First Commandment 'Thou shalt have no other gods before me'.[7] One God means one power, one presence, one life eternal. As we acknowledge no other power and recognize that sin, disease, lack, and limitation are not powers but shadows of belief, without presence, power, jurisdiction, and without government or control, as a matter of fact, without entity or identity, we are seeing and understanding God as the great universal Principle of all existence. From there, we go to the second great Commandment which Jesus gave, 'Love thy neighbour as thyself'.[8]

When you and I begin to understand that every word that appears in Scripture is a universal truth and is therefore the truth about all being, and that any other appearance—whether appearing as enemy or friend—is the illusion of sense, and that *I and the Father are one* is the universal truth about all beings, then we can love our neighbour as ourselves.

[7] Exodus 20:3.   [8] Matthew 19:19.

CHAPTER XVI

THE UNIVERSALITY OF GOOD

THE twelfth chapter of the Gospel according to John opens with the Master coming to Bethany, where a supper has been prepared for him by Mary, the sister of Lazarus whom Jesus had just raised from the dead. Naturally, the little town is very much excited about Lazarus being raised from the dead —Lazarus present with them now and even eating supper after having been dead and in the tomb.

We might well imagine that this occasion was one for rejoicing, for happiness and a real celebration, but that is only because we want to believe that the whole world is seeking truth and wants to see the dead raised to life and sinners reformed. The world as a world does not really like such things; it harbours an unconscious resentment towards those who have any desire to improve it. And so, the first murmurings of discontent are heard, and soon these murmurings become more than murmurs, rising to greater heights. This, the Master fully realized when he prophesied the trouble that lay ahead:

Verily, verily, I say unto you, Except a corn of wheat fall into the ground and die, it abideth alone; but if it die, it bringeth forth much fruit.

John 12:24.

Here is the very principle on which The Infinite Way unfoldment is based. Translating that into our language of today, it means this: Unless we die to our humanhood, we cannot be reborn of the Spirit, nor can we bring forth spiritual fruit while continuing to live as human beings.

Most people do not have any real understanding of what living the spiritual life means, and so when they first start out on the spiritual path they usually feel this way: 'I am a human being, one who knows nothing of God, and I am sick. My desire is to be a human being who knows something about God, and who is well.' They seem content to stay on the level of demonstration, wanting to be free of all their human discords, wanting to acquire all the good human things of life, and to continuing merrily on their human way to the age of three-score years and ten, or a few beyond, and then pass on as mortals normally do.

For years and years, that seemed to be my understanding of the purpose of metaphysics in this age. It was only as the years went on that I began to discern that actually we were using truth-teachings only as another form of *materia medica* and that practitioners were being thought of merely as people who healed rheumatism, tuberculosis, cancer, or arthritis, but simply by using a different method from that of the doctors. We prayed, we knew the truth, we did a daily lesson, and ultimately found that our sinful habits or our disease had left us, or perhaps our supply had grown a little more abundant. In place of fifty dollars a week, we earned a hundred dollars and some even became millionaires through the study and application of truth.

Comforting as it is to be a healthy human being, satisfying as it is to be a wealthy human being if one has enough intelligence to know what to do with the wealth after he gets it, that still is not the goal for those who seek spiritual illumination. There still remains the question: What does it mean to live the spiritual life? The answer to that question lies in Jesus' revelation:

'Except a corn of wheat fall into the ground and die, it abideth alone: but if it die, it bringeth forth much fruit.'

He that loveth his life shall lose it; and he that hateth his life in this world shall keep it unto life eternal.

John 12:24, 25.

Had the Master continued just healing sick people and feeding poor people, he might have gone down in history as a great

L

philanthropist and healer, but certainly not as the Saviour of the world. Similarly, if we attempt through spiritual work to hold on to the humanhood into which we were born, if we think of our spiritual practice merely as a means of becoming better, healthier, or wealthier human beings, we shall lose our life and come to the same end as all humanity—the grave. Some come to it early in life, some in middle years, and some in very late years, but all humanity ends in the grave.

Death, or passing on, is not an advanced or progressive step, unless a person passes on while on a progressive, upward, spiritual path. Then even if a person does succumb through some human error in the form of accident or disease, that one error or failure to realize the presence of God will not prevent him from very quickly re-establishing himself on the upward spiritual path. The person who really is on the spiritual path, even though he fails in one particular situation to realize God's grace and may therefore pass on from disease or accident, will not find that to be a barrier to the ascending consciousness. It will be only a temporary stopping place, quickly overcome. He will pick himself up, and then that which is often said about those who have passed on will become true in his experiences, for now, at last he knows the truth, has found a release, and is really free.

Those who use truth merely for some personal end have not yet caught the first glimpse of what the Master meant when he gave us this great teaching, a teaching so great that one could take those two just quoted from John and probably write a dozen books on them. Those books would have to explain what really cannot be said in just a few words—that even good humanhood, even wealthy or healthy humanhood, is not spiritual life. Material living and mental living are two strata of one thing, and that one thing is materiality, but spiritual living is something that does not find any counterpart in the human scale. Spiritual living is an entirely different realm, as different from the human level of life as electricity is from gas or gas from whale oil. They are different areas, different types of power, just as spiritual living is an entirely different universe and level of consciousness from the material.

He that hateth his life in this world shall keep it unto life
eternal.

John 12:25.

This does not mean hate in our sense of the word *hate*. But
it does mean that we must learn to recognize that any degree
of human living is not the spiritual life, and that we must be
willing to see the human sense of existence fade from our consciousness, so that the spiritual sense of life can come in, and
when that happens, we are ready to be raised into the realization of the Christ.

This teaching of the Master does not mean that we are to
die and then find life eternal because to succumb to death
means to become more deeply enmeshed in mortality and
materiality. It means that we are to begin to *die daily*, now
and here, to those things which we have heretofore considered
objects of demonstrations—to stop being concerned over
whether or not the body is complaining of something at the
moment and stop being satisfied when the body says, 'I am
entirely well', or when our income jumps to a hundred or a
thousand dollars a week, or some other sum that seems to meet
our every need. Let us not be satisfied, because that is death to
our spiritual development.

Our work should be the realization of Spirit and its fruitage
in spiritual living. Certainly, we will still appear to the world
as normal human beings. We will still be so many feet tall and
so many inches wide; we will still enjoy food and the con-
veniences of modern life, but our heart will not be in those
things. They will just be the comfortable things of daily existence, the *added things* of demonstration, but not the *objects* of
demonstration.

Now is my soul troubled; and what shall I say? Father, save
me from this hour: but for this cause came I unto this hour.

John 12:27.

This is the Master speaking, but does he really mean that he
is asking to be saved from 'this hour', since that is the purpose

of his whole demonstration? Then he follows with: 'Father, glorify thy name.' That is the secret:

'Father, glorify thy name.' Show forth the glory, the health, the harmony, and the eternality of Thy being as me, as my experience, not to glorify me, not to show forth how healthy or wealthy I can be; but glorify the name of God, the nature and character of God by showing forth all that God is—all the harmony, all the perfection, all the eternality and immortality which is of God. Show that forth as my individual being.

This spiritual practice is not for the purpose of showing forth the understanding of the spiritual healer, but rather the harmony of God made evident as individual health and wealth.

Every healing from this basis demonstrates the infinite nature and character of God made evident as our individual experience. And so our health is really the perfection of God made manifest individually as the health of our body. Do you see the difference between that and your or my having a healthy body or a great understanding? We do not have great understanding; there is no such thing as your or my great understanding. God alone is infinite perfection, and all we can do is show forth the perfection which is God. Whether we express it as understanding, as health, or as wealth, it is still the activity of God being made manifest—the Word becoming flesh and dwelling among us.

'Lean not unto thine own understanding. In all thy ways acknowledge him, and he shall direct thy paths.'[1] Let us always realize that we are not showing forth the understanding of a man, but the Spirit, the eternal life which is God, expressed as our individual being. In the twelfth chapter of the Gospel according to John, we glimpse the humility and dedication of Jesus, showing forth not his understanding, nor his demonstration, but as a living witness to all that is of the Father made evident as Jesus' individual experience. And to what purpose? That we might learn the principle and go and do likewise.

And what is this principle? That we must give up our

[1] Proverbs 3:5, 6.

personal sense of life—in scriptural language, *die daily, hate* our human sense of life. In other words, we are not to cater to it, nor desire that it be made a little healthier or prolonged a few more years, but rather turn away from the physical sense of life that we may achieve the spiritual consciousness which is life eternal.

Then came there a voice from heaven, saying, I have both glorified it, and will glorify it again.

John 12:28.

I, God—I, the very life of our being, always glorifies Itself by expressing Itself as our perfect life.

The people therefore, that stood by, and heard it, said that it thundered: others said, An angel spake to him.

John 12:29.

And in our individual awareness, sometimes we hear it as if It were the still, small voice just whispering in our ear; sometimes It thunders; and at other times It is merely a sensing or stirring within us.

Several years ago, somebody called me for help as I sat dictating my mail, and just for a moment I closed my eyes, which is my usual listening attitude. It seemed as if God were actually whispering in a voice that said, 'Your thinking can't change anything'. And I had such a sense of release that that ended it. That's how it comes—just a still, small voice, but there are times when it can thunder in our ears, too.

Jesus answered and said, This voice came not because of me, but for your sakes.

John 12:30.

The Master himself knew that the physical sense of life is not life eternal. When he stood at the grave of Lazarus and said that it was not for his sake, but for the people's sake that he prayed God that Lazarus come forth, it was because he did not need any prayer to God; he did not even need to issue a command for Lazarus to come forth. As far as he was concerned, life is, and always has been, eternal and eternally manifested, so it was only a concession to public opinion when he let them think that the dead Lazarus was being restored to life.

Few people are ready or willing to believe in miracles. Even the people who saw Lazarus raised from the dead, even those who had been fed in the wilderness, even the multitudes who were healed, did not believe. The moment the test or trial came, they were willing to walk away—even those who had benefited by the healing ministry of the Master. This applies not only to the people of that age; it applies to the people of every age.

When a person enters into spiritual work as a practitioner, teacher, or lecturer, he is presenting the Christ, the Christ living and omnipresent; he is presenting the idea of the very immanence of God. Therefore, no one engaged in a spiritual ministry can permit himself to be built up, since he has had nothing to do with attaining the Christ except to become aware of It, and then to have the willingness to share It. Those who do permit themselves to be built up and to develop into popular personalities end on the cross. There is no way to prevent this because that is the nature of human experience.

We are not here to glorify the personal self, since the personal self can of its own self do nothing. Jesus knew that it was the Father within who did the work. Paul recognized that same thing when he said that he could do all things through Christ. Every mystic and every person of spiritual insight have come to learn that the Christ, or the realization of the presence of God, can bring forth water from the rocks; It can make manna come from the skies; It can multiply the loaves and fishes—but no man of himself can do those things. All power is given to us through God, through this Christ.

The people deserted the Master, and the Master quoted Isaiah who prophesied this very thing:

He hath blinded their eyes, and hardened their heart; that they should not see with their eyes, nor understand with their heart, and be converted, and I should heal them.

John 12 : 40.

All those still enamoured of the desire for improved human-hood will want to keep their eyes closed; they will not want to see this Christ that takes away what appears to the world as ease in matter. Even though it is only a temporary stripping bare, they resist it, because it is so comfortable to go on in their good, healthy, wealthy, human way. So humanhood will always want to turn from the Christ.

Nevertheless among the chief rulers also many believed on him; but because of the Pharisees they did not confess him, lest they should be put out of the synagogue :

For they loved the praise of men more than the praise of God.

John 12 : 42, 43.

Is it not almost unbelievable how history repeats itself throughout the ages? 'They loved the praise of men more than the praise of God.' This means that until we come to that place of *hating* our human sense of life, we want not so much the praise of man as the demonstrations of man. Probably we want these demonstrations for praise; probably some people like to have it said that their metaphysical understanding has brought them a Cadillac instead of a Ford, or that it has given them a healthy body. Thus, they would rather have the praise of men than to forego the Cadillac or the healthy body and seek the realization of God.

'For they loved the praise of men more than the praise of God.' We all have to watch that we do not fall into the danger of wanting the praise of men. We must translate or re-interpret our desires and actions to see if we want something of men more than something of God, if we are not wanting a little more of the human comforts rather than that spiritual life which transforms the entire being. On that point hinges our spiritual demonstration.

'What went ye out for to see?' What is it that we are seeking? Is it human good in one form or another? Is it human comfort of one kind or another? Is it anything of a human nature? If so, there are many ways of achieving it, but following a spiritual teaching is not one of them. This spiritual path is a path that may not for the moment give us all the material demonstrations we are seeking, but when we have achieved, recognized, acknowledged, and attained an awareness of the Christ, then all the *things* are added in greater degree than ever we thought possible when we were trying merely to demonstrate them.

Jesus cried and said, He that believeth on me, believeth not on me, but on him that sent me.

And he that seeth me seeth him that sent me.

John 12:44,45.

That sounds like a paradox, it sounds like a mystery; but actually it is not. It is as clear as a bell, because it brings out the point that if we are thinking of the human Jesus, we are missing the mark in praising him or believing on his name— missing the mark entirely. As soon as we begin to see the principle that God is made evident as an individual, we can then believe on any individual who is a transparency for God because we have recognized that God constitutes individual being and that that individual is the showing forth of all that God is.

'He that seeth me seeth him that sent me.' We see Him if we are not looking too sharply at this body. It is when we look at the I of a person that we see the Father that sent him. Let us always differentiate between looking at the body of a person or looking at the person and thinking we are seeing him. We see the person only when we look behind the eyes, and there see the light that is being made manifest as individual being. When we do this, we are seeing 'him that sent me'. Then we shall not be tempted to believe on any human being, but we will believe on the I, the Word, the Life, made manifest as individual being, since this universal Principle not only appears as a Jesus, but as any and every John, Bill, or Mary in the world.

I am come a light into the world, that whosoever believeth on me should not abide in darkness.

And if any man hear my words, and believe not, I judge him not: for I came not to judge the world, but to save the world.

He that rejecteth me, and receiveth not my words, hath one that judgeth him: the word that I have spoken, the same shall judge him in the last day.

John 12 : 46-48.

God is not mocked! Truth is not mocked! Truth is the judge. We cannot mock truth any more than we can mock the principle of mathematics. If we continue believing that 2 x 2 is 5, the very principle of mathematics itself will take its toll of all those 2 x 2's that come out 5—I know that from experience with my own chequebook. God is not mocked. Principle is not mocked. But it is not a man who judges! It is the violation of the principle itself that takes its toll of us.

For I have not spoken of myself; but the Father which sent me, he gave me a commandment, what I should say, and what I should speak.

And I know that his commandment is life everlasting: whatsoever I speak therefore, even as the Father said unto me, so I speak.

John 12 : 49, 50.

In other words, Truth revealing Itself as and through this individual reveals the bread of Life. We are free to take It or leave It. The decision is not a difficult one—just whether we are to use Truth for some personal purpose in life, or whether we are to develop a consciousness in which we permit Truth to use us and permit the Father to speak His words and have His way through us. That is the difference, and that is what accounts for the difference in demonstration.

'In my Father's house are many mansions.'[2] There are many states and stages of consciousness, many states and stages of awareness, many states and stages of demonstration. It is not

[2] John 14 : 2.

for you or me to kick against the pricks or to complain if our progress is slow because, if we do, some day when the progress is too fast, we will also complain that we are being pushed ahead too rapidly and made to do and say things that the world is not ready for. Then, it would seem as if we could cry out, 'Father, Father, hold me back. This is too much for me. This is too strong meat.'

Let us not complain at this period if we seem to be slow in going forward. Let us not complain later when the going gets rough, and the impulse, the drive from within, is so strong that it does not let us have much sleep at night, or much rest by day.

All of these things come to those who have embarked on the spiritual path. It is the old story being relived. 'Ye have not chosen me, but I have chosen you.'[3] When that call comes and God takes possession of our consciousness, we are compelled to take forward steps that oft-times we wish we did not have to take. We are compelled to say and do things that we know right well outwardly may be misunderstood. That is not for us to say any more than it was for the Master to pray the Father that this hour be removed, when this was the hour for which he came:

Except a corn of wheat fall into the ground and die, it abideth alone: but if it die, it bringeth forth much fruit.

John 12 : 24.

[3] John 15 : 16.

CHAPTER XVII

WHOLENESS OF SPIRIT

IF the universality of the Christ were understood, one church would never be judged as better than another or as nearer the kingdom of God, nor would anyone think that belonging to a certain group, sect, or organization in some way entitled him to benefits of God which others could not enjoy. To an enlightened state of consciousness, that is nonsensical.

The Christ is as available to sinner as to saint. He 'sendeth rain on the just and on the unjust'.[1] The Master exemplified this teaching by his willingness to heal the woman taken in adultery, and the boy born blind: In no wise, did the Master distinguish between saint and sinner, except to caution the sinner to 'sin no more'.[2]

The Master's teaching does not encourage anyone to sin. It merely reveals that the Christ is ready and omnipresent to lift us out of wherever we may be, whether in sin, in disease, in lack, or in prison. And the activity of the Christ which can lift us out of these conditions would so change our consciousness that never again could we return to that same state of sin or disease, lack, or limitation, or a life of crime. Once a person has received the benefits of God, that which caused him to sin should have been eliminated.

Understanding the manner in which the Christ acts to transform consciousness, and therefore our experience, calls for quite a different capacity than being able to grasp the value of thousands of dollars worth of property or investments, or to be aware that we have a healthy body and are able to enjoy it. A recognition of the Christ requires a different state of consciousness because here we are dealing with that which is invisible and intangible to the finite material human sense, what Job

[1] Matthew 5:45.   [2] John 5:14.

referred to when he said, 'He . . . hangeth the earth upon nothing'.[3]

A doctor can easily understand how he can remove a pimple or a growth, and he knows of course what medical steps are necessary to remove infection from the blood. But it is a very difficult thing for a doctor to understand how someone can sit in a hotel room in San Francisco and through prayer remove these same impurities of the blood from somebody half a continent away in Chicago. Material sense cannot conceive of such a thing as possible because material sense is built on concepts of time, space, height, width, and depth; and when a person is out of the realm of these tangible measurements, he has nothing left to cling to because that is all that material sense is composed of, and that is all that it can understand.

There is Something, however, that is not included in time and space, that has neither height, width, nor depth, and yet is so real that It can provide food for the multitudes—fish and loaves of bread—It can provide healings of any form of sin and disease for the multitudes; It can take a person out of poverty and raise him into a state of affluence.

That sounds like Aladdin's lamp which, through a person's wish made the intangible become tangible to sense. But we have gone further than wishing or desiring; we are at the place in consciousness where we accept as real, omnipresent, and all powerful that which we can never see, hear, taste, touch, or smell. Either that state of consciousness is an incredible and impossible one, or we have touched some great reality of which the world has no knowledge.

The Christ is the Spirit of God appearing as our individual consciousness. The Christ is an ever-present power and a reality, and even though It exists as that which can never become tangible to the five physical senses, nevertheless it does appear tangibly as food, transportation, home, and companionship.

The Master's experience at Jacob's well in Samaria illustrates this point. He was talking to the woman of Samaria and had asked her for water. The conversation had progressed to the point where she asked him how he could produce water.

[3] Job 26:7.

since he had no bucket. And then he told her that if she knew who he was, she would know that he could give her water that would be a wellspring of eternal life; and 'whosoever drinketh of the water that I shall give him shall never thirst'.[4] This water to which he referred was the infinite, invisible Principle which could appear tangibly as water, as inspiration, or as the spiritual awareness, which it did, because she immediately recognized him as the Christ.

When the disciples offered to bring meat to the Master, his answer again was in a similar vein: 'I have meat to eat that ye know not of.'[5] The meat he had was this meat of the Spirit, this realization of the Christ, this awareness of the omnipresence of good, and he knew that even if he missed his luncheon and many more meals he would not feel depleted from any lack of food. Here was another evidence of the Infinite Invisible, this Christ which is intangible to human sense, but which appears visibly as meat, as sustenance, or as rest.

It is this very Spirit which enables those on the spiritual path to eat less food and sleep fewer hours than they did while they were wholly in the material sense of life. This Spirit feeds the very body with what the world calls food, and yet it is an invisible food; it supplies the body with rest, even while the body is not lying on a bed in unconsciousness. One can be wholly conscious and about his work and receive the same rest that others receive in sleep—probably an even higher sense of rest.

The one thing necessary in order to receive this invisible expression of an invisible Substance is the ability to discern the Christ where a human being seems to be. Humanly, we look out through our eyes and see men and women—children and adults, white and black. But when the spiritual sense is attained, all we are consciously aware of is the child of God, the very presence of God made manifest. There is no division in one's thought about whether it is male or female, or whether it is young or old. There is the realization of all as being one in Christ. That is the recognition of spiritual wholeness which is the ability to realize, not separateness—not separate men and

[4] John 4:14.   [5] John 4:32.

women, not separate people with separate interests—but the one divine Love made manifest as individual being.

This does not mean that we lose our individuality. Rather do we gain more individuality. The more of God that appears through us, the greater the degree of what the world calls individuality. Sometimes it is called personality, but every quality attached to a person as personality should be understood as some phase or facet of God shining through, and not as some personal quality of that individual.

When Jesus said, 'I have not spoken of myself'[6] . . . he that seeth me seeth him that sent me',[7] he was not raising himself up to Fatherhood. He was eliminating the personal sense of self, showing that the Father is all, and that the individuality of God is infinite and appears infinitely. If you or I show forth any qualities that the world considers desirable, let us at least give God credit for being the Source, Foundation, and Reality of whatever those qualities may be. Above all things, let us not hide our personality or our individuality, but realize once and for all that it is the infinite, invisible God appearing outwardly to the world as whatever qualities of character or appearance we may have.

We live in a practical world of cold, hard facts! There are bills to be paid requiring money with which to pay them; there is the space between our home and office, and at the present time that space must be travelled by means of automobiles, trains, aeroplanes, or ships. We are in a practical world where food must be paid for and all the everyday routine experiences must continue to go forward, since we are commanded not to leave the world. Jesus did not say that we would be taken out of the world—we would be in the world, yes, but not of it.

In the world, it is necessary to conform to the ways of the world, at least in the sense of eating, drinking, and sleeping, and paying for that eating, drinking, and sleeping. Therefore, we engage in all the activities in which the world engages; commerce, art, industry, healing work, publishing work, printing—all the practical things of life. But we do these things with this difference. We do not look to our own cleverness, our

[6] John 12:49.   [7] John 12:45.

own education, experience, or inheritance: we look to the Christ, the infinite, invisible Spirit within us to lead us in every rightful way and direct us in just the activities which we are to perform at the moment.

For example, if I am to appear on a platform at any given time, there must be an inner guidance to bring me there. Then, I find those who are ready and prepared for this particular mission. If I should leave the Infinite Invisible out of my calculations, I might have recourse to some of the world's ways, like advertising, and have ten times more people than otherwise might be there, but in that event there might be only one-tenth the number of people capable and willing to receive and respond to this message. But Christ recognized, acknowledged, and listened to, operating in, through, and as individual consciousness brings those together who are all on the same path, of one mind in one place, seeking the same unfoldment. They may come from widely different backgrounds—Jews, Protestants, Catholics, Mohammedans, Hindus, Confucianists, Taoists—but regardless of what their backgrounds may be, when they are drawn together by the Christ, they are of one mind, one spirit, and one intelligence, all imbued with the ability to understand and receive this message.

So it is that the Christ operating as your consciousness has led you step by step to this hour and to this book, and that Infinite Invisible in you will continue to operate and lead you as far as you can go—if necessary to the fullness of the Christ-mind. Teachers and teachings are only temporary expedients, landmarks of unfolding consciousness on the Way.

Every spiritual message is received directly from the Christ because the Christ is always with us. Does that mean from a man who lived in Galilee two thousand years ago? No, the Christ that taught in Galilee as Jesus of Nazareth was teaching 2,000 years before that and is teaching today. That state of consciousness appears and reappears throughout history. At one time, it may be known as Moses; another time, as Krishna; another time, as Jesus Christ; and today, as one of our modern spiritual teachers.

The state of consciousness made manifest to the world as

Abraham, Isaac, Jacob, Isaiah, Elisha, Elijah, Jesus Christ, John, and Paul is our individual consciousness, only awaiting our acknowledgment of Its wholeness. We acknowledge it in part every day when we turn within expecting and receiving a healing of a headache, rheumatism, or a cold through Its activity. If the claim is a little more severe or serious to the world sense, we call upon a practitioner. We do not expect the practitioner's flesh and blood to do anything for us. It is his degree of unfolded consciousness, a degree of consciousness higher than our own or a clearer transparency than our own, although that, too, is still the Christ-consciousness.

If we are dedicated and sincere enough, that state of consciousness unfolds within us until we can deal with a claim regardless of its name or nature or degree, and that makes of us practitioners, and ultimately teachers. And what has brought this forth? Only one thing—the mind that was in Christ Jesus, and this in proportion to our degree of unfoldment of it. It is possible to walk on the water, actually, physically; it is possible to walk through the wall, actually, physically; but it takes a higher degree of this unfolded consciousness than we have yet attained. There is no denying that a mighty measure of that Christ-consciousness has already been attained—an earth-shaking unfoldment of it witnessed. The metaphysical world today is performing healings that could have been believed only in the time of the Master, and performing them through that same mind that manifested itself in Galilee except that now that mind appears as your practitioner or mine, as your teacher or mine.

The Christ, then—this Immanuel, this presence of God—is the mind that was in Christ Jesus,[8] and as It fed the multitudes then, so It will feed the multitudes now. But you and I must begin in an individual way. Each day, we must give recognition and acknowledgment to this Christ, even though It is invisible, even though we cannot see It, hear It, taste It, touch It, or smell It. We must recognize that we are never alone because the Father is always with us.

The Christ is omnipresent, and It goes before us and acts

[8] Exodus 14:13.

within us as wisdom, as our protection and counsellor. It is all things to us in all our ways. It is the reality, the actual force of being. It is a mighty power, and yet it is not a power of might but of the Spirit. This is the same Power which Moses recognized when he said, 'Fear ye not, stand still, and see the salvation of the Lord'. It is the Power which we recognize when we are called upon for help and hear the still, small voice when it says, 'Don't battle that disease; don't battle that sin. The battle is not yours, but God's.'

The Spirit of God in us, this Christ, is the master of all situations. It is the dispeller of the illusions of sense, regardless of whether the illusion appears as sin, disease, or death, or whether it appears as a sinful person, a diseased person, or a dead person. The one thing that dispels the illusion is this very presence of God which we recognize more in stillness and in quietness than we do in mental jugglery. Only when the human senses are quiet can we become aware of the still, small voice, only when we have learned to refrain from battling an error which has no real existence, only when we have acknowledged that, regardless of the sin or the disease before us, it really does not exist, since God is infinite good and can never be responsible for that which appears as these erroneous pictures.

Once we have recognized the nature of error to be nothing but mental pictures, illusions, mirages, or suggestions, coming to us either for acceptance or rejection, we have come to the point of the Christ, which recognizes there is no need to fight, there is no need to spend a thousand dollars advertising for work and for customers. 'Stand still, and see the salvation of the Lord !'

If divine Wisdom reveals the need for human footsteps, we take them, but we will find that in taking them we are not taking them foolishly or unwisely. We are not spending days and days knocking at doors; instead we are led quickly to the right place at the right time, even to the right advertisement. What human footsteps we take are under divine guidance, and then we have less of them to take, and no footsores with them !

This consciousness of truth develops and unfolds through

M

practice, yet the declaration of truth does not bring it into existence. It requires practice; it requires a reliance on It and a trusting in It even in what may seem to be very adverse circumstances and situations that may take time to solve. Yet standing in this Truth gradually brings the light of the Christ-presence, and that comes through devotion to the practice of the Presence.

It is necessary for each one to make the decision whether he is to serve God or mammon, whether he is to serve the human sense of existence and battle it out on that level and be successful, or whether he will find a rest from mental and physical struggling and let this Christ take possession of him and his affairs. We never take possession of It. We never use Truth. We never use God. We never use Spirit. It is the Spirit that touches us, transforms us, and then picks us up and does for us all that is to be done. The great mistake is in believing that we can continue to be human beings, living a completely materialistic life and at the same time have some great knowledge of the Spirit.

In the degree that we remain human beings, in that degree are we lacking the understanding of Spirit. It is when we *die* daily to the human sense of power, the human sense of intellect, and the human sense of understanding, and become imbued with the Spirit that we go out and become active in the world. And once we are touched by the Spirit, it is impossible to be lazy mentally or physically. The Spirit will not give us rest. It will not give us peace while we are doing nothing! This is not a do-nothing teaching. This is not a let-God-do-it teaching. This is an actual opening of consciousness to the presence and power of the Christ, until It, the Spirit, touches us and makes us new again. When It does, the new life begins.

CHAPTER XVIII

GOD OMNIPRESENT AND THE
ONLY POWER

MOST people come to a study of truth seeking release from the cares and the ills of the world, and for a while it is a very satisfying experience to know that all manner of problems can be met through spiritual power by means of prayer.

To receive healings, especially if *materia medica* has declared the disease to be serious or fatal, is a never to be forgotten experience by those who have had them. I know what this means because after the First World War, I was told that I had less than three months to live. There was no known cure for my trouble and there was nothing that *materia medica* could do to save me. As a matter of fact, in all the years that have passed since then no cure has been found for that particular disease. Nevertheless, in spite of this verdict, in three months I was so completely healed that there has never been a sign or trace of the trouble in all the years since 1921.

I have had many other healings through the Spirit, and I have witnessed thousands of healings—true, many of them minor claims, but also some very major ones according to *materia medica*. Undoubtedly, many of you have had similar experiences with disease or with sin. It was in 1928 as I was sitting with a practitioner that all my smoking, drinking, and card-playing habits disappeared. These were not great vices, but nevertheless they were errors according to the spiritual way of living, yet they all disappeared in that one two-hour experience, never to return. Not only did a healing of smoking, drinking, card playing, and a few other minor human errors take place, but illumination came—a lifting of consciousness above what we might call the earth plane, and never in all the years that have gone by since that time have I completely come down to earth again. This does not mean that there have not been many problems during that time—many. But I have learned that all of them were a part of my own development.

As the years unfolded, there came a lessening of satisfaction in business, and soon after that illumination in 1928, I began the practice of spiritual healing, and by 1930 this had become my life work. At first, it was very satisfying and even exciting to sit down with sick people and see them lifted back into health or to be called to someone who was dying, to sit with him a while, and then greet him in the office a few days later. In those early days, this was an experience that came frequently, because in my youthful innocence I did not know how it was done, and that made it simpler and easier to accomplish. It was just necessary to sit quietly, to be at peace, to feel the presence of the Spirit, and then shortly thereafter to hear from the patient, 'I feel wonderful!'

But after a while, there came this thought: 'I wonder what I am doing in this work. Am I becoming just another kind of doctor? Am I here just to heal people's headaches or colds or flu or cancer? And why? What is so wonderful about stopping somebody's pain or setting him free from some ill so he can go back to his human ways of living? After all, to continue this way is merely to give people a few years of no pain or a few more years of experience here on earth. Evidently, all I am doing is helping people to change the dates on their tombstones!'

Then this new unfoldment came to me, and healings began to be brought about not merely for the sake of the healing, but as a part of spiritual regeneration. My attention began to be centred more on opening the consciousness of people to the realization of the presence and power of God, and the ever availability of God. This brought a greater sense of peace and joy in my work, and although the healings continued to occur, no longer were they associated, at least in my thought, with just turning pain into ease, disease into health, or lack into abundance. Now it seemed to me as if I were more nearly fulfilling the teaching of the Master who specifically told us to take no thought for our life, that it was the Father's good pleasure to give us the Kingdom, and that in seeking the king-dom of God, all these things would be added unto us, and there-fore, it would be futile to run after them, trying to demon-strate or achieve them since they were going to be added with-out any effort—if and when we found the kingdom of God.

In working along that line, the next question that presented itself was this: Is this spiritual power something that can be utilized only for the benefit of an individual, or is it something that can be made available to the world? And it was while studying the life and works of Buddha and especially the passage in which he told of his desire to do something about the sin, disease, and death in the world that a great light dawned in my thought. He indicated that at no point did it occur to him that he should cure people of their sins or diseases. The only thing that registered in his consciousness was: Is there a principle that will eliminate sin, disease, and death from the world?

What a tremendous idea that is! Is there a principle that will eliminate sin, disease, and death from the world—not is there a principle or law that will heal this one or that one, but is there a principle which, if its operation were understood, would remove sin, disease, and death? From the moment this idea entered my consciousness, it became my prayer and my meditation. From then on, I sought a principle which not only would heal people, but would actually take sin and disease out of the world.

Without question, Buddha did discover that principle. His illumination revealed the principle that there is no sin, disease, or death, that these are not realities, but are mere beliefs in human thought which, when recognized as such, disappear. Buddha did remarkable healing work, and so did his disciples—until his teaching was organized. That ended this great work.

Whether that principle has been rediscovered in this age and whether it will operate to rule sin, disease, and death out of human consciousness, only time will tell. It may take several generations before we have any concrete evidence on this score. But whether we recognize it or not, we have come to a new place in our individual experience. There are conditions today, just as there always have been, which promise evil and destruction to the world. It matters not whether one thinks that this destruction will be brought about by socialism or communism, by some political party, or by an atomic or hydrogen bomb. That is not important. The point is that any of these, or all of them, are at the present time suspect, and that people throughout the world are beginning to fear them. There is great fear in the world—fear of another war, and especially fear of atomic of germ warfare.

With all this fear is also the opposite side of the coin. People are beginning to talk of spiritual power with which to overcome the atom bomb, the next war, or the next depression. Articles are appearing in newspapers and magazines to the effect that nothing will stop the coming catastrophe except spiritual power. Even people who know nothing about metaphysics are talking about spiritual power as a possibility, as a matter of fact, as the *only* possibility of preventing these horrible and greatly feared disasters facing the world.

It is comforting and satisfying to read about spiritual power, to be told that in this age greater advances will be made in this area than ever before, and to know that more and more people are turning their thought to spiritual power. But no one has as yet told us what that power is, and how we are to utilize it.

What is this thing called spiritual power? How do we go about using spiritual power to prevent atomic warfare or to overcome its effects? How do we go about bringing spiritual power to bear on our problems? How does it operate? And who is to do the operating?

Before we arrive at the point where spiritual power really does these remarkable things, some of us will have to know a great deal more about it and about how to bring it into our experience, than we now know. Most of us have already been witnesses to spiritual power because the healings which have taken place in our experience have come about through spiritual power usually brought into experience by a practitioner, although occasionally a person is able to work out his own problems by himself. More often than not, however, the practitioner does the work, and the patient merely says, 'Thank you; that was beautiful!'

But just what is this spiritual power that is brought into action to heal a disease or to overcome a sin? To say that it is the power of God would be just as mystifying as to say that it is spiritual power. That would be true. It is the power of God; but there again, what is the power of God, and how does It operate? Spiritual power, a power that is based on the realization of the allness of God, actually is the realization of the *unreality* of that which appears as the power of disease or the power of sin. The conviction and realization of the unreality of the appearance is the way in which spiritual power becomes evident as healing.

Every sect or denomination in the world will tell you that God is all, that God is everything, that God is all-power. And yet those statements have not healed disease except in the rare instances where the spiritual counsellor was himself of a very spiritual nature and through his own developed consciousness —not through the teaching of some theological doctrine or through declaring God to be all, but through his developed consciousness—has caught some degree of the Christ, and It did the healing.

It was only when the principle of healing was revealed by metaphysics that healings took place, not just hit or miss or when some spiritually developed soul came along and performed healings, but with regularity as the result of the application of a principle, a rule or a law. This principle of healing is based on the allness of God, but the allness of God is never brought into actual demonstration except in proportion as an individual comes to know and realize the nothingness of what appears as sin or disease.

To the human senses, disease is very real. Some forms of it can be seen by the naked eye, whereas others are visible only through a microscope. And yet, spiritual power reveals that there is no power in that disease, that the power exists not in the disease itself, but in the *universal* belief or fear of the disease.

If a single spiritual healing has ever taken place in the

history of the world through the realization of the nonpower of that which appears as infection, contagion, or germs, if even one case has been actually healed through that awareness—and of course we all know that there have been millions of such healings—then a principle has thus been discovered, and that principle is the nonpower, the unreality, of all that would appear to sense in the form of what we call error, sin, or disease. That is spiritual power.

If that is true—and I am one who believes it so firmly that I spend my life living only for that purpose—then it becomes necessary for each one of us in some measure and in some degree to realize that whatever forces are in operation in this world that claim to have power to produce evil, death, lack, or limitation are not power.

It is probably true that more plotting and planning of the destruction of human society is done ignorantly than viciously, but it is vitally important for us to know that the human thought throughout the world that plots and plans evil, either consciously or ignorantly, is not power. It is not always the Machiavellian schemer that the world has to fear. There are so few of them and their power in and of itself so small, even from the human standpoint, that they are not the ones to be feared. It is the ignorant do-gooders, the ignorant dupes, who become the tools of evil. In their effect on the world, they are as powerful as infection and contagion are in the realm of disease.

Nobody well grounded in spiritual wisdom would ever deny that infection and contagion are not serious threats in the world, when believed in by the human world. All one has to do is to remember the many flu and polio epidemics to know that these human beliefs operate as law and act to produce their own image and likeness. But spiritual treatment has proved that these infections and contagions are not power, and now it is our duty to prove to the world that world beliefs of a political nature, a governmental or an economic nature, which threaten to be as disastrous as an epidemic, are also not powers.

Anyone who has experienced the healing of a contagious or infectious disease is a witness to the fact that infection and contagion are not power. Those housewives who have at one time or another burned themselves with hot water or sizzling fat in their kitchens and have proved the painlessness and the healing of these burns are living witnesses to the truth that the laws of matter are not laws. They are beliefs, and they are nullified the moment one with God, one with Truth, realizes that what is appearing as sin or disease, infection or contagion is not law and is not power.

When we talk about spiritual power, we are talking about the power of a consciousness imbued with the truth that only that which emanates from God is power, that only that which emanates from the divine Love or the divine Principle of the universe is power. That which men set up as power is not power at all—it is not even law. It operates as such and it acts as such, but one in this truth is a majority. So, when a spiritual healer imbued and inspired with this truth comes into a neighbourhood, he sets up an immunity by realizing that error in and of itself, in whatever form it appears, is not power, is not cause, and cannot produce anything. The only power it has lies in a person's reaction to it.

As long as there is a belief in our thought that God is some mysterious power that is going to cure disease or heal or reform sinners or that God is going to overcome some form of error, we are not imbued with spiritual power. It is not enough to know that God is all and that God is love. It is not enough to go around singing hymns of praise about God and to God.

Spiritual power is the realization that God alone, Good alone, Spirit alone is power; and that anything that appears in the form of human experience is not power. Nobody can be imbued with this power until he is fully convinced that this is true. But until he has arrived at an understanding of the nothingness of what appears as error, has realized this truth in the healing of a cold, a headache, a corn, or a bunion, and gone on further and further until he has seen cancers, tuberculosis, and tumours healed, until he has seen entire sections of certain communities healed, he has no right to go to others, to talk about the healing of national or international evils.

The atomic bomb cannot drop itself; a war cannot declare

itself; a panic or depression cannot come about of itself. It takes the thoughts of men to produce these disasters. The question is: Is human thought power? Is human thought capable of such evil? The answer is: Yes, it definitely is—just as germs spread disease—until one with God comes along to become a majority, one who understands that human thinking, whether individual or collective, is not power.

People of developed spiritual consciousness recognize that human thought is not power. Human thought is an avenue of awareness, but it is not power. All the thinking of all the people in the world could not change a coat button into a diamond; All the world put together could not *malpractice* one person into sickness, unless that person wanted to give up his sovereignty of thought and say, 'Yes, yes! I give my body over to you! Go ahead and make me sick! I believe you have power over me'. The person who gives his consent can be *malpractised* but not the person who knows the spiritual truth that God gave man dominion over the sea and over the air and over the water and over all the things in and on and above the earth. Knowing that one truth would free him of malpractice because if he knows his God-given dominion, he is free.

Jesus' great prayer was that the Father should glorify him with His glory. Can you imagine being glorified with the Father's glory and then having someone give you a headache simply by thinking or wishing you were sick? Let us be through with such nonsense! The human mind is an avenue of awareness. Through our human thinking, we can become aware of a person's presence, but no amount of human thinking ever known can bring anybody to us. The only thing that can do that is the realization of the omnipresence of God, and that is not bringing somebody to us: It is realizing he is already here.

When the Hebrew prophet's servant thought that the enemy was too strong for them, his master prayed that great prayer, 'Open his eyes, that he may see'. And when the servant's eyes were opened, he saw that 'the mountain was full of horses and chariots of fire'.[1] Elisha's prayer did not put those warriors

[1] II Kings 6:17.

there; thinking did not do it; but through the inspired consciousness of the prophet it was evident that they were already there because of God's omnipresence. That is what put them there—God's omnipresence. So the inspired prayer of any individual can open his eyes to the truth of the omnipresence of God, appearing as dominion, purity, Life, Truth, Love, Soul, and Spirit.

The important point is: Can we, through knowing the truth of God's omnipotence be so at-one with God, and thereby such a majority that we can nullify all vicious and ignorant human thought so that it will not operate as the experience of the people of the world? We are a very, very small group. All the metaphysicians in the world are a very small group, but they may be great enough to overcome this belief that human thought is power if they can understand the truth that God alone is power, rather than merely hoping, wishing, or believing it is true.

After more than thirty years in this work, I can testify that healing is more successfully brought forward through knowing that human thought and human hatred are not power, and that jealousy, envy, malice, or resentment cannot create anything, than through any other form of treatment I have ever known. These qualities are shadows of a belief without anything to sustain them but our own fear of them and our own acceptance of them as power. Whether that hatred is in our thought towards someone else or in someone else's thought directed towards us, it has no power.

As we are able and ready to accept this great truth of God's omnipotence and omnipresence and to realize that all that masquerades as human thought, human will, human desire, lust, greed, and animosity are not powers, we are readying ourselves for the experience of the Christ.

What is this Christ that we may enjoy individually, and if individually, ultimately prove collectively? The Christ is an experience that any one of us can have, and can have at will, at any moment, any day, any week. The Christ must be made to live in your experience and in mine, but the Christ must be made manifest through our *conscious* desire, through our *con-*

scious effort, through the *conscious* activity of our daily living.

The great mystery is that God is the mind and consciousness of individual you and me—God is your mind and mine; God is your consciousness and mine. We do not have to go up on a cloud to find God. We do not have to contact or become at-one with a far-off God. God is here where we are. Right here and now, God is the Soul of us and the consciousness of us. Without this understanding, we have no hope of bringing forth the Christ into our experience, since then we would be looking for It where It does not exist—out here, separate and apart from our own being.

If, even intellectually, we come to the knowledge that Scripture is true, and that God *is* love, not a love outside us, but the love that is expressed by us here where we are, that God is mind, not a divine Mind somewhere out there in space, but the mind of my being and yours right here, then we have taken the first step towards the demonstration of the Christ. The Christ is that state of consciousness—yours and mine—when the hate and the fear and the love of error have been removed. If in the tiniest degree we can lose our fear of error —whether it is the fear of human thought or human emotion, whether it is the fear of somebody else's wrong thinking or of our own wrong thinking, whether it is the fear of universal mortal thinking, or whether it is the fear of infection, contagion, lack, or of limitation—if in a measure fear can be removed from our consciousness, in that degree is our consciousness the Christ-consciousness.

When we attain the fullness of the Christ, we can walk on the water because we no longer have any fear of sinking or of losing our lives. The only reason we do not walk on the water is the belief that we have a life to lose, but when once we have lost the idea that we have a life of our own and really come into the realization that God is our life, we will walk on the water without fear of drowning.

As we lose our fear of this world, as we become convinced of the truth of the Master's words to Pilate, and when we can respond to our particular Pilate—whether it be sin, disease, lack, limitation, or lonesomeness—with Jesus' words, 'Thou couldest have no power at all against me, except it were given thee from above',[2] in that measure are we developing our sense of the Christ.

The Christ, being our very own consciousness, appears to us in tangible form. In biblical days, It appeared as manna from the skies and water flowing out of the rocks; It appeared as a few loaves and fishes, and as tax money in the mouth of a fish. Today, it appears as food, clothing, housing, right activity, companionship—even as unimportant a thing as a parking space. What are these experiences but demonstrations of the consciousness of the Christ appearing in tangible form, appearing outwardly as the form necessary at the moment?

That is where our good comes from—from the depths of our own consciousness. And if we do not have any depths to our consciousness, it does not come. Probably much of it eludes us because we do not know that it comes from within, and we are waiting for it to come from outside. We may even think it is going to come from our practitioner or teacher, but it is not. It wells up from the depths of our own consciousness.

Once we realize God as our consciousness, we can expect anything to flow forth into expression, anything that we need at the moment. Out of that consciousness comes our safety and our security. Out of our own consciousness, we find ourselves safe in the secret place of the most High, dwelling in the consciousness of the Christ-truth that the Pilates of this world are not power.

When we read about spiritual power, we must always remember that we are not reading about a power that somebody else is generating to protect us. It is a power inherent in our own consciousness which, as we recognize it, will come forth as our Ninety-first or Twenty-third Psalm. The world is in trouble today because it accepts the belief that God is in the sky above, instead of the teaching of the Master that the kingdom of God is within us. The world is looking everywhere but *within* for the kingdom of God.

There is only one place of safety; there is only one place of security. It is not in the Bibles with steel plates in them that

2 John 19:11.

were sent to the boys at the front. It is not in any human document or in any human form or in a human power. If we are expecting it to come from a material or human source, we are looking for it in that which heretofore has destroyed the world, because the same material force and power that we look to, to save us one day, we expect will destroy the enemy the next day.

There is only one place to find safety, security, and peace, and that is in spiritual power. Spiritual power is the power of individual consciousness when we realize that human thinking, human planning, or human scheming is not power and that it cannot reach any further than the minds of those who are planning and plotting it. In other words, it can destroy only itself.

Somewhere in the world there must be those who are prepared to go one step higher than attempting to use God to heal their bodies or to increase their income. Somewhere in the world there must be those who are willing to listen to the Master when he says, 'He that findeth his life shall lose it : and he that loseth his life for my sake shall find it'.[3]

Let us understand that if we are trying to preserve this thing we call our human sense of life, we are merely preserving that which ultimately will go anyhow. We are not preserving it; we are pickling it for a little while—that is all! There is only one way of preserving it and that is through the realization that Life is God—God is life, indestructible and eternal. All the ignorance of truth in the entire world cannot destroy that which is God.

As our fears are erased and as our consciousness opens more and more, the Christ appears. The Christ is that spiritual consciousness which appears in whatever form is necessary to our unfoldment and demonstration. The Christ is your consciousness and mine when that consciousness has given up fear for itself and for the world, when it has given up the belief that human thought has power—that hate, envy, jealousy, or malice can produce anything, even disease or war.

What difference does it make whether we credit the human

[3] Matthew 10:39.

mind with the effect of disease in our body, or whether we believe that the human mind can bring about a war? It is all a belief in the power of the human mind. And there is no denying that the human mind does have that power in the world until one with God comes along—and those of us on the spiritual path have to be that one.

Mysticism is the revelation of an infinite Presence and an infinite Power, of an all-presence and an all-power which is our own consciousness. It is not a far-off God. It is the Kingdom within us.

Spiritual power is the realization of this truth, but in order for it to work for us we have to become conscious of this truth. It is no different from a checking account. A checking account is dead; it cannot move; it cannot write itself out; it cannot spend itself out. Unless we ourselves have a conscious awareness of that checking account—the amount, its purpose and power—it is of no use to us, just as the money in our pocket is of no use except in proportion to our conscious awareness of it, of its value, and of its presence.

So it is with God. God is omnipresent; God is omnipotent. God is all-power; and God is all-in-all. But what good is that knowledge to the people in hospitals, asylums, and the graveyard? The allness of God is made manifest only in the degree of a person's conscious awareness of that truth. That is why there are spiritual practitioners and workers. They are exactly like other people in the world, but with this difference: They have gained a little greater conscious awareness of God's allness and error's nothingness. That is all that makes practitioners, and the only thing that makes a practitioner a good practitioner is his awareness of the allness of God, and the nothingness of what appears to the world. If a practitioner were to become frightened at some pain or at the appearance of disease or at sin in a patient, there would never be a healing. Healings occur only in proportion to the practitioner's lack of fear, and the reason a practitioner does not become frightened or overcome by fear in the face of these errors is because of his conviction that what is appearing as a horrible condition is illusion, not reality, not power—not cause and not effect.

This knowledge we have to carry out into the world and use in meeting world problems. We are dealing with human thought—vicious human thought on one hand, and ignorant human thought on the other hand. Add it all together and it is still human thought. As human thought, it has power only to the world that accepts human thought as power. But it becomes null and void when it meets truth, the truth of God's order, of Love's order, of Life's order, of Intelligence's order. And when it does that, it is touching the Christ of our being, and then the Christ appears as safety, security, peace.

The acceptance and realization of this truth in our consciousness will operate as the Christ of our experience; and regardless of what happens in the world, we will be kept free of danger, discord, or destruction. This is not being selfish because in doing that for ourselves it may follow that we are doing it for a friend or a relative. We do not know how far it may reach out to the peace and political tables of the world to settle the affairs that are being debated at those tables.

This too is revelation! If our world were destroyed, if humanity were wiped out, if civilization went crashing into ruins, a remnant would remain. That remnant would be those of Christ-consciousness because they will never be destroyed. The sons of God are never destroyed—they cannot be. Spiritual consciousness cannot be shot; spiritual consciousness cannot be buried in a tomb. Therefore, if you and I and one, two, a dozen, or a thousand in the world have developed some degree of spiritual consciousness, we shall certainly be spared the experience of destruction, and a new civilization can be built upon the spirituality that remains in your consciousness and in mine.

Reality is never destroyed. God, the one Life of the world, will never be wiped out—and that Life is your individual life and mine, and the lives of millions we have never heard of. Even if humanity appears to be wiped out, not one individual Soul or one individual consciousness will die. As a matter of fact, in reality, there has never been a death since the beginning of recorded history, and that is because there has never been more than one Life in heaven or on earth, and that Life is God. It is indestructible, whether It appears as your life or mine, as the life of Jesus Christ, or the tree outside. Life is indestructible because Life is God, and any appearance to the contrary is automatically wiped out.

As we individually here and there realize that truth, we prove, not the immortality of God—we do not need any proof of that—but the immortality of your life and mine and of your body and mine. We must remember that when Jesus Christ came out of the tomb, he came out with his selfsame body, the very body that had been crucified. The very body that appears right here is indestructible! It will never be put into a grave regardless of any appearance to the contrary. And one with God—one with Truth—is the saving presence.

God is the very consciousness of your being and of mine. Christ is our very own consciousness, and that Christ appears tangibly as whatever form is necessary to our experience—food clothing, transportation, immortality, eternality, or whatever is needed. *Christ appears as that form.*

CHAPTER XIX

GOD, THE OMNIPRESENT REALITY

FREEDOM of health in Christ and freedom of supply in Christ are entirely different from freedom in the body and freedom in the purse, and yet health in Christ manifests itself as physical freedom, just as freedom of supply in Christ manifests itself as an abundant purse. We lose all sense of tension when we realize that our health, wealth, and happiness are not in these forms, but that our freedom is of the Christ as we open our consciousness to Its inflow:

Christ is imparting Itself eternally as my consciousness, and I am receptive to this Consciousness which is the embodiment of all that is. All that is, is good, and since God made all that was made, I am the very embodiment of that good. I am the state of receptivity as which that infinite Being is expressing Itself.

As individual consciousness, I am responsive only to the Christ, and nothing can enter that consciousness to defile or make it a lie. There is only one Consciousness, God, and that is my individual consciousness now.

As we meditate on this truth of receptivity to the Christ, we shall find that all the Christ is pours Itself forth as our individual consciousness.

'And now, O Father, glorify thou me with thine own self, with the glory which I had with thee before the world was.'[1] It makes no difference whether it is a truth-message, whether it is selling or buying, manufacturing or farming. The thing that counts is that what we are doing is animated by the Spirit and vitality of the Soul.

[1] John 17:5.

If what we are doing carries with it this spiritual spark, it will prosper, it will succeed, it will make glad, it will make happy, it will satisfy, and it will be of good report. Spirit always satisfies. Spirit always fulfils Itself; Spirit always completes Itself in success. The important point is not what work we are doing, but whether we are doing it from our own limited sense of self or whether there is a Spirit permeating the activity and carrying it out.

This principle is exemplified in the life of Elijah. The Hebrews had been persecuted, and they were killing even their own prophets, and one of these, Elijah, had been driven out into the wilderness. There, he had the experience of being taken care of in mysterious and miraculous ways—mysterious and miraculous only to human sense, but not to Christ-consciousness. In his understanding of the Christ, it was perfectly normal and natural that, wherever he found himself, all that he required would appear in the form needed, whether food, clothing, or protection. But that there must have come to the thought of even this God-centred man some doubt about the ultimate success of his mission is recounted in that scene in which the still, small voice speaks to Elijah, telling him that God had saved out a remnant of those who had not bowed their knees to Baal.

Here was a man with a holy message and with nothing to do with it—no place to give it, no one with whom to share it. And in that moment of seeming failure and discouragement, the Voice told him that there was a remnant ready to receive his message, which points up another principle of our work. Regardless of what we may be doing, there is always a remnant to provide the people necessary for our particular activity—a congregation, customers, patients, or clients. Whatever our activity may be, as long as it expresses God-qualities, as long as we introduce into our work the divine idea of service, beauty, harmony, joy, peace, satisfaction, perfection—good in any form —as long as our work partakes of the nature and qualities of the activity of Intelligence and Truth, then we, too, can know that there has been a remnant saved out for us.

To find our freedom from lack, limitation, and discord, our

work is first to find that freedom in Christ. Freedom in Christ means to be imbued with the Spirit, to have all that we do imbued with the activity of the Soul. It is the practical application of the Master's teaching: 'I can of mine own self do nothing';[2] and of Paul's, 'I live; yet not I, but Christ liveth in me'.[3] When we embody in our work this idea of the Spirit performing all that we are called upon to do, when we open our consciousness to a receptivity to the Christ so that It animates all our activities, giving us wisdom, guidance, direction—what the world calls intuition—It leads us into the right way and into doing the right thing at the right time.

It is true that there are many people who have been successful without bringing any thought of the Spirit or the Christ into their activity. They have done it by means of hard work, and often their careers have ended with either physical, mental, moral, or financial difficulties of a serious nature because the human mind is such that no matter how great it becomes, there is always the possibility of its reaching a breaking point. Only when the Spirit animates our human activities can they be perfect and eternal, and then the divine Presence goes before us to make the crooked places straight.

Certainly, there is such a thing as physical health. There are people who have never known a pain or an ill in their entire lives, but this does not mean that they are healthy. It means that for the moment—for that day, that year, or for that ten, twenty, thirty, or fifty years—they are enjoying a sense of bodily health which may change at any time into disease or death. Such is the history of the human world. Only when we realize that Spirit is the health of the body and of the mind, only when Spirit is the animating principle of all our activities, only when we look for our health in God instead of in the body, do we find real health. And when we find it, we have a better sense of health and of youth and vitality than we knew even when we had what was considered a healthy physical body.

We are dealing with a spiritual universe and a spiritual body, but we are dealing also with the world's false concept of

[2] John 5:30.   [3] Galatians 2:20.

that spiritual universe and spiritual body. Our body is a
spiritual body; it is the temple of the living God. God made it.
God made all that was made, but only as we understand that
God is individual consciousness can we understand that God
really formed the body.

This could be proved very quickly and easily, in a sense at
least, if we decided that for the next twelve months we would
keep our thoughts high in God and our consciousness on the
level of Christ, Truth, Spirit. If such a decision could be carried
into practice faithfully, at the end of a year when we looked in
a mirror, there would undoubtedly be a different look on our
faces, and probably even a different appearance to our bodies.
This ought not to be too difficult to believe because surely no
one would dispute the fact that if for the next twelve months
a person were to dissipate in every way possible, we would un-
questionably see a body and face showing forth great changes.

In other words, the state of consciousness that we maintain
is expressed in the body that we present to the world. Our consciousness has formed and forms the body. A change of consciousness begun today can create an entirely new body within
ten years. No one would recognize his own body ten years
from now if for the next ten years he were to live, move, and
have his being in God-consciousness. Similarly, if he went on a
ten-year period of wild dissipation, we know right well what
he would look like.

If we would maintain our identity as Christ-consciousness
for a period of one, two, or ten years, we could transform the
entire mind and soul and body of our being. And we would
transform the body of our business and our home life. Everything concerned with us would be changed in just a few years
if we maintained our consciousness on the Christ-level and did
everything as out from the Christ, being a witness always to the
fact that the Christ is the animating principle of our mind,
body, and business. Actually, it is our own consciousness that
formed our body in the beginning—even before we were con-
ceived—and that is why it looks like you or like me and not
like anybody else.

Consciousness in its pure state is God, but we have accepted the universal belief that this consciousness is personal to us, and therefore our experience has been limited to that personal consciousness which is comprised of our heredity, environment, education, and individual experience.

The longer we hold to the belief that body, business, health, and marriage show forth our personal consciousness, the longer we shall experience limitation in all those directions. When, however, we give up that belief for the truth that God alone is individual consciousness, then our body, business, health, wealth, home, and family will show forth, not the results of a personal, limited, finite consciousness, but the infinite Consciousness that we call God. That is how we bring about the transformation in our experience.

All of us have accepted the universal belief at some time or other and to some degree or other that we are showing forth the fruitage of our education or lack of it, our good home environment or lack of it, our past business experience or lack of it, and as long as we continue in that strain, every area of our experience will express limitation.

There is nothing to prevent us from beginning at any moment of our career—this minute if we like—to accept the truth that God is divine consciousness, that this Consciousness is the consciousness of individual being, and that our daily experience is the outpicturing and outflowing of the divine Consciousness that is God.

Sometimes, we may find ourselves wondering, 'What is my goal on this spiritual path? What is it I am seeking?' There are many answers, of course, because the answer depends upon where we are on the path when we ask the question.

The first answer may be, 'I am trying to get rid of a disease'; or, 'I am looking for a bigger opportunity in life'; or, 'I want more money'; or, 'I want more satisfying companionship'; or, 'I want a better relationship in my home'. But as we advance further and further on this path, the answer changes. We begin to realize that what we are seeking is God, the peace that passes understanding, and life eternal.

When we are in our twenties and thirties it is not too unnatural to have a desire for health and money, but by the time we reach our forties and fifties, we are beginning to think about life eternal because the human span seems to be drawing to a close and we do not like to face such a prospect.

At one stage of this quest, my idea of immortality was like that of many others. I thought of it as an increased number of years, in other words, longevity. I thought that if I could live to be one hundred or one hundred and fifty, I would, by that very lengthening of years, be experiencing more and more immortality. I know better now. I have come to see that immortality or eternality is a present possibility. Not only is it a present possibility, but it is a present reality, despite the fact that we are not yet fully aware of it.

Just as the consciousness that I am, produced and formed my body before it was in the womb, just so the consciousness that I am will be forming my body and my experience into eternity. 'Before Abraham was, I am' . . . I am with you alway, even unto the end of the world.'[5] Think of the word I. Just say I, and remember that that I existed before Abraham, and that that I will exist unto the end of the world. Then you will begin to achieve, not merely believe but achieve, a measure of immortality expressed.

The secret is in the word I. That I is independent of body. That I is not encased in a body at all. That I is universal and merely appears here on earth as body. If you were looking at me, it would seem that I am body—but I am not body at all. What you are looking at is not I: What you are looking at is my body. I am back of my eyes, invisible to your eyes. And that I of me is God, but that I of you is also God. It is God individually appearing as you and as me, and because God is infinite, God must be infinitely expressed as your individual life and mine. And that is why that I that was before Abraham was is the I that I am and the I that you are.

Many of you, I am sure, have had some experience in the mystical life, that life in which we consciously feel our oneness with God. Those who have had even a small degree of such experiences have had some awareness of their pre-existence. They know, not only that they lived before their birth on this

[4] John 8:58.   [5] Matthew 28:20.

plane, but sometimes they know even how and where they lived and remember some of the experiences that took place before what is called human existence. With the mystic illumination also comes the realization that they are infinite and individual, and yet always they are God manifesting Itself in infinite varieties of form.

Our experience is determined by whether we accept the human sense of consciousness, or whether we accept God as our consciousness. Whatever we may be doing, if we are looking to our own experience, environment, or education, we will be limited, not only as to what we are doing, but as to the fruitage that comes from what we are doing. The moment, however, that we open our consciousness to this idea that God manifests Itself in Its infinity, we are no longer limited. Then, we hear that still small voice that Elijah heard, telling us that God will save out a remnant for us in our work, just as the Voice told Elijah that God had saved out for him a remnant of those who had not bowed their knees to Baal.

In other words, God, the Source of all divine ideas, has provided those who are to utilize His ideas. Therefore, if you are sure that your work carries with it some activity of divine grace, beauty, holiness, harmony, service, intelligence, or love —any of these qualities—then it comes from God. The whole activity is of God. The government is upon His shoulder, and God Himself must and will provide the capital, skill, customers, or students.

Our purpose in being on this path is not merely to give us better health or greater longevity, nor to bring in more dollars. Our purpose is the expansion of consciousness to the point where we recognize God as our individual consciousness, and therefore good flows out from that divine Source in infinite measure.

That is our real mission in this work. If we can *die daily* to limited human belief and be reborn in and of the Spirit in the realization that we are never limited to a human mind, a human experience, or a human consciousness, but that God is our consciousness, then It may flow through in an entirely new life, flow forth in new work and new activity, or it may increase and prosper the one in which we are now engaged.

Spirit knows no limitation. Spirit just pours Itself through. It comes flowing through in such a wild, rushing manner that we can hardly believe it is possible when It begins. We are beholders, and it is almost as if we were watching God work over our shoulder, as if we were just watching the activity of God and wondering at Its munificence, Its beauty, Its bounty.

The moment you watch God reveal Itself as your experience, you will be surprised and astounded to see the infinite ways as which God can appear. I am not referring particularly to dollars. Dollars are really the least part of our experience. True, they are abundant enough for all our needs, but that is the least important part of it. It is the beauty, the vision, the broadness, the joy—those are the things that will astonish you. Your consciousness, when you know God to be your consciousness, is infinite, and infinite things will flow forth from it.

We are on the spiritual path for but one purpose: to *die daily* to our human sense of life that was and to be reborn to the life which is God; to *die daily* to the limited finite sense of ourselves that we have always entertained, and be reborn of the Spirit, to realize Spirit as our true identity—and then watch and see how It unfolds. Then we may see a business man become a religious teacher, a schoolteacher become a painter, a housewife a poet or a musician.

Anything can happen when the Spirit is free, and when we are free in Christ:

In Christ, I am, infinite; in Christ, I am that point of consciousness through which all of God shows Itself forth. Only in Christ can that be; only as the Christ can that be—not as person, not as limited self, not as somebody with a human history, but only as I turn from my human sense of life and find my freedom through the realization that God is individual consciousness and that God is pouring Itself forth as my individual experience.

'My conscious oneness with God constitutes my oneness with all spiritual being and things.'[6] God, the divine Conscious-

6 Joel S. Goldsmith; *Conscious Union with God* (London: L. N. Fowler & Co. Ltd., 1960), p. 223.

ness, is unfolding, revealing, and disclosing Itself as my individual being. God appearing as my individual consciousness automatically constitutes my at-one-ment with every spiritual idea and being, whether it appears as a person, place, thing, circumstance, or condition, since the Consciousness which is God must be all-inclusive and include every idea, every person, every activity, every thought, and every formation.

As infinite Consciousness, I embody and embrace within my own being every right idea, and that must continuously flow forth as my daily experience.

If this were true about one person and not true about every person, the entire mission and message of the Master would be for nought, for then we would be at the place where again we would be worshipping a man. But the message and the mission of the Master is that this is a universal law. He refers to God as your Father and my Father. There is only one Father, and that Father is the universal creative principle appearing as you and as me.

This Consciousness which is God is the consciousness which formed your body before it was in the womb. You are not a finite limited person building a body for yourself; God, the divine Consciousness, has built the body for you, and that body is His, regardless of how sick or deformed it might look to your eyesight at this moment. If you could see this body through spiritual discernment, you would see it in its infinite perfection and in its eternal and immortal growth.

Let us never forget that this very body which we see so finitely when we look in the mirror and which looks to us as if it needed so much correction and improvement, this very body is the temple of the living God, only we are looking at it through the old eyes of personal sense instead of through the new eyes of spiritual vision, the first Adam-eyes, instead of the last Adam-eyes. Instead of looking in a mirror to see ourselves, we should close our eyes and then we will see the body as it really is.

Every person who has ever been responsible for a spiritual healing has had the experience of seeing the spiritual man and spiritual body. Spiritual healings cannot take place in any other way. It is only as we close our eyes, figuratively speaking, to the human scene that that little inner spot, that spiritual corner of our being comes into play, and all of a sudden it realizes God manifest, it realizes the meaning of spiritual man and spiritual universe, spiritual being and body, and then a healing takes place, whether it is our own, a patient's, a relative's, or a friend's.

Spiritual healing is accomplished through spiritual discernment, and in no other way. And what is it that we are to discern spiritually? The temple of God, the Temple not made with hands, eternal in the heavens. That Temple is our body; that Temple is our business; that Temple is our home; that Temple is our universe; and it is a Temple not made with hands, not made with thoughts: It is the creation and the emanation of the divine Consciousness of our individual being when we acknowledge God to be our consciousness.

The unfoldment of our experience is up to us. We ourselves are responsible for that. We could be charitable and say that when we are ignorant of this truth, our experience is limited, finite, sickly, sinful, and coarse, because we are not aware that God as our consciousness appears as our daily experience.

But from the time that we touch even a little of spiritual wisdom—more especially, the moment that we enter the consciousness of those who are spiritually illumined—we have no more excuse for finiteness and limitation in our experience. We then must accept our responsibility and agree that what we are next year will be determined by what we can accept of truth this year, that our demonstration is our individual problem, and that we ourselves can remove the limitation from our experience—true, in a measure only, because this comes bit by bit, but we can begin to unfold spiritually as soon as we are convinced that God is our individual consciousness, and God, Consciousness, unfolds, reveals, and manifests Itself as our individual body, business, home, and daily experience.

From the very instant we draw on God as our consciousness, we are drawing on Infinity, and bringing forth infinitely. The first step on this path is, of course, the intellectual agreement that this is true. But that intellectual agreement will not carry us very far. From that point on, there has to be a specific action on our part because nothing happens to us except as the activity of our individual consciousness. In other words, if we just slide by each day without some new activity of consciousness, then we cannot expect our experience to be any different next year from what it has been the preceding year. If we are to bring something new into our world during this next year, we have to begin with this moment and continue each moment with some conscious activity of consciousness.

There is no such thing as sitting by and saying, 'Well, I am going to let Consciousness do it; I am going to let God do it'. Yes, we are going to let Consciousness do it, and Consciousness will do it, but only in proportion to our conscious co-operation.

The greatest and first step in the direction of this opening of consciousness to Truth is learning to take not less than three periods of every single day for silent prayer or meditation. Three times a day at least, and ultimately four and five and six, sit down for one minute, or two or three—it does not matter how short a time or how long a time you give to it; the idea is that some conscious activity takes place which may be described as receptivity. As a matter of fact, it might prove so simple that you achieve it even while driving your automobile, or riding in a streetcar or bus. It is as simple as touching your ear to indicate that you are opening consciousness to the inflow of this truth—just opening the ear, or sitting down for a moment in silence and realizing, 'I am receptive to the Christ'; or, 'I am a state of receptivity to the Christ'; or any little thing that you may do which will open your consciousness to that inflow.

This must be repeated three, four, or five times a day to keep the flow open because there is a mesmerism out here in the world. Every time you read a newspaper or listen to the radio, a little more of that hypnotic suggestion of a sinful world, or a fearful world, of a diseased world is thrown at you, and because of that constant pouring in and hammering away of world beliefs there must be some counter influence, and that counter influence is your conscious receptivity to the Christ. It has to be an activity of consciousness, specifically, definitely, consciously. You may either sit down, stand up, or walk, but open that inner ear and realize your receptivity to the Christ.

In proportion as you do that, you have the beautiful experience of being able to sit down in the morning and at night and for five or ten minutes find yourself in a state of peace, and in that quietness begin to feel the inflow of the Spirit as it courses through the whole body. This is a real experience, an actual one. Many people in this work have had, and do have, a continuous experience of the Spirit pouring Itself through; but It flows more easily and quickly in silence than in speech. Speech sometimes stops it. The more of silence there is, the more power there is in the words when they do come forth. Silence is of tremendous power when silence is linked with receptivity, with that listening ear.

It is a 'Speak, Lord; for Thy servant heareth';[7] or the prayer of the Hebrew prophet Elisha, 'Open his eyes, that he may see'.[8] That prayer is not asking for more warriors, more help, more supply—simply, 'Open his eyes'. And what happens when the servant's eyes are opened? Then he knows that even the clouds round about are filled with warriors. And so we, too, find that the streets round about are filled with customers, employers, employees, students, patients, or an audience—whatever is necessary to our unfoldment at the moment—but not if we pray for these things, because the truth is that these things are already here. Health, wealth, harmony, opportunity, peace, joy, power, dominion—they are all right here. Our consciousness is full of them. There is only one thing hiding them—the mesmerism of this world, and to see through that mesmerism takes inner eyes.

There are those who have ears but do not hear, and those who have eyes but do not see. That is what I mean. We have eyes, certainly. But do we see those hidden warriors? Do we see this infinite supply of good? We cannot see them with our human eyes; we see them only with that inner eye, when our attention is centred on receptivity to God.

In that inner vision, we can behold everything present now.

[7] I Samuel 3:9.   [8] II Kings 6:17.

It is all here. We do not need to have a single new thing added to our experience to make it complete: We have only to open our spiritual eyes to see the fullness and completeness of God's universe, which is already here and which is already now— and then the world is new.

GEORGE ALLEN & UNWIN LTD

Head Office:
40 Museum Street, London, W.C.1
Telephone: 01–405 8577

Sales, Distribution and Accounts Departments
Park Lane, Hemel Hempstead, Herts.
Telephone: 0442 3244

Athens: 7 Stadiou Street, Athens 125
Auckland: P.O. Box 36013, Auckland 9
Barbados: P.O. Box 222, Bridgetown
Bombay: 103/5 Fort Street, Bombay 1
Calcutta: 285J Bepin Behari Ganguli Street, Calcutta 12
Dacca: Alico Building, 18 Motijheel, Dacca 2
Hong Kong: 105 Wing on Mansion, 26 Hankow Road, Kowloon
Ibadan: P.O. Box 62
Johannesburg: P.O. Box 23134, Joubert Park
Karachi: Karachi Chambers, McLeod Road, Karachi 2
Lahore: 22 Falettis' Hotel, Egerton Road
Madras: 2/18 Mount Road, Madras 2
Manila: P.O. Box 157, Quezon City, D–502
Mexico: Separio Rendon 125, Mexico 4, D.F.
Nairobi: P.O. Box 30583
New Delhi: 1/18B Asaf Ali Road, New Delhi 1
Ontario: 2330 Midland Avenue, Agincourt
Rio de Janeiro: Caixa Postal 2537–ZC–00
Singapore: 36c Prinsep Street, Singapore 7
Sydney: N.S.W. 2000: Bradbury House, 55 York Street
Tokyo: C.P.O. Box 1728, Tokyo 100–91

Also by Joel Goldsmith

The Infinite Way

WITH AN INTRODUCTION BY JOHN VAN DRUTEN

In this small volume the author sets down the spiritual truth as he has gleaned it during thirty years study of the major religions and philosophies of all ages, and fifteen years of practical application of truth to the problems of human existence—health, happiness, family life, business and security. 'It teaches you to look away from your problems instead of at them, and in doing so to find their solution.' From the introduction by John van Druten.

Living the Infinite Way

In his earlier book, *The Infinite Way,* Joel Goldsmith demonstrated the need for individual prayer and meditation in the realisation of the God experience—the recognition of the activity of God within us. He writes about the means of living the Infinite Way. He discusses the nature and power of prayer; and the necessity for recognising that the acceptance of God's omnipresence requires the suspension both of opinion and of dependence on appearances. The author contends that at any moment we can begin spiritual sowing and immediately begin spiritual reaping.

The Art of Meditation

Starting from the conviction that man is not alone in the world, Joel Goldsmith is concerned with man's need of prayer. Prayer—the art of meditation—has to be developed and he introduces the reader to a daily programme of meditation which will help him to realize his oneness with God and to find a clearer view of himself and his world.

GEORGE ALLEN & UNWIN LTD